Autophagy And Fasting Step-By-Step Guide

Michael Angelo Delbuono

Dedication

To my wife, Lori, and my three beautiful children Amanda, Mikey, and Cody.

Acknowledgment

I would like to acknowledge all the people who supported me throughout this book and those who evaluated every aspect of it. My family and friends who believed in me. It is because of their constant support and trust that I was able to break through and achieve this milestone.

My heart truly belongs to you.

Thank you.

About the Author

Michael Angelo Delbuono is a health practitioner who operates on the domains of autophagy and a healthy lifestyle. He strongly believes that the true way of living a healthy and nutritious life is to train your body as well as your mind.

Throughout his life, he has advocated the benefits of autophagy, and how it plays a huge role in our life in combating several illnesses, obesity, and potential health threats. This book is his masterpiece, where he informs the readers about the abundant advantages of autophagy and the science behind it.

Preface

Autophagy is not just another diet in the market to influence bloggers, fitness enthusiasts, or celebrities. It is a lifestyle. It is a healthy habit that you willingly indulge in and make the most of throughout your life.

Regardless of its simplicity and easiness, autophagy comprises several unique sequential steps – transport to lysosomes, degradation, and utilization of discarded products – as each step may differ from the other.

The process of autophagy is quite different from other extracellular processes. Three types of autophagy – macroautophagy, microautophagy, and chaperone-mediated autophagy are discussed thoroughly in the book along with promised advantages and long-term benefits on your health.

Contents

Page Left Blank Intentionally

Chapter 1
Introduction

One of the biggest problems we face today in this progressive world is the lack of nutritional food included in our diets. The world is changing rapidly, and so are our habits with each passing year. The world has progressed tremendously over the years, and it has directly affected the way of our living in one way or another. We lead a much comfortable life today, thanks to the invention of newly formed gadgets. Instead of walking longer distances as people did in the past, we have invented cars and bullet trains to help us reach our destinations within the timespan of mere minutes.

The electronic devices we use today help us connect with people who live far away from us. The list of our advancements seems to keep increasing. There is no end to the possibilities in this world, and we have made it our mission to push beyond our limits in this world. Every other invention was made to provide us with more comforts, but today we are facing more drawbacks than we could ever imagine. With the invention of such gadgets, we have also created a world where we barely have time for ourselves. These advancements may have their own advantages, but every advantage in this world comes up with a disadvantage on the side. Otherwise, the word 'advantage' itself would lose its meaning. And we, humans, are all about trying to keep the meaning intact in every field of life.

Regardless of which country, city, or nation we belong to, all of us are busy trying to catch up with the pace of this world. Sometimes it feels as if this world is getting ahead of us, and we have to keep running in our lives so that we are not the only ones who are left behind.

Time has become scarce to the point where we cannot even catch our breaths or momentarily take a break from our busy schedules. Living such a fast-paced life in a world that is continuously progressing has led to a number of problems that we overlook today.

These problems are often overlooked only because none of us really have the time to catch a break and allow our minds to wander toward things that matter the most. We have inhabited these problems in our lives and have made them a part of our lifestyle. One of the most problematic habits we have developed today is eating food that provides us with minimal nutritional value. We are constantly searching for numerous ways to make cooking a quick process just to satiate our hunger. From microwavable foods to fast-foods and to junk-foods, we have come up with quick remedial methods to 'save time' at the expense of sacrificing our nutritional health. We opt for fast food because we tell ourselves that we do not have enough time. Most of the time, we get lazy while preparing our food after having a hard day.

We tell ourselves that we can spend the time we *waste* on cooking food by doing some other important task without realizing how important meal preparations really are. What is the point of saving your time if you are cutting down your lifespan with the intake of food that provides you with zero nutritional value? What is the point of saving your time if you are not going to spend it in the future?

Sometimes, we eat junk food in order to fulfill our 'cravings,' and sadly, for most people, junk food is the only type of food they can afford on their budgets. However, we all need to realize that the food we eat has a direct impact on our bodies. You are what you eat, and if you have picked up this book, then it probably means that you want to eat healthy. We all know what happens to our bodies when we eat unhealthy food. Fat starts depositing in different parts of the body, and there is a visible change in our physical appearance. But what matters the most is the chemical changes that take place inside of our bodies. We widely believe that the only process that takes place in our body due to the intake of less nutritional food is the deposition of fat. That is where our misconceptions lie, and these misconceptions can have adverse effects inside your body as you try to look for numerous ways to get rid of that fat.

There are a number of biological processes involved in every mechanism of life. This book solely focuses on the autophagy diet and the effects this diet will have on your body. Before we can talk about autophagy diet and what it really is, it is crucial for us to understand the chemical processes that take place inside of our bodies.

Types of Organ Systems

The biological processes take place around the various organ systems present inside the human body. We all know that the human body is composed of various organ systems that work together to help us function properly. There are a total of eleven organ systems inside our body that perform specific functions and work together. Each system involves a certain type of biological process that helps a body function properly.

Circulatory System

It involves the biological process of circulating blood around the body through the heart, veins, and arteries. The main function of this system is to provide oxygen and nutrients to organs and cells. It also involves the function of excreting the waste products from the blood vessels and helps to keep the body temperature in a safe range.

Digestive and Excretory System

Our main focus in this book involves these two organ systems that work together and help us excrete the unwanted waste from our bodies through the process of retaining the important nutrients in the body. The digestive system involves the gastrointestinal tract. The GIT includes the mouth, esophagus, stomach, and intestines.

Endocrine System

It helps regulate the proper amounts of hormones required inside our bodies.

Integumentary System

This organ system involves the skin, hair, nails, sweat, and different types of glands in our bodies. These glands regulate and maintain the hormones that are secreted inside our bodies.

Muscular System

This part, in particular, involves the system of muscles that enables the body to move.

Immune System

The main function of the immune system is to defend the body against pathogens that can enter it and endanger the lifespan of useful cells inside of our bodies.

Nervous System

The nervous system deals with collecting information from different parts of the body to the brain and vice versa. The information travels from senses to nerves present inside our bodies. Nerves are a network of fibers that transmits impulses of sensation to the brain. The impulses travel from the brain to the muscles and organs. The information reaches the brain and directs the muscles to contract so that it can command the physical actions to be taken by the body.

Renal and Urinary System

These two types of organ systems work in filtering the blood through the kidney and producing urine to excrete wastes.

Reproductive System

This type of organ system involves the sex organs for the production of a baby.

Respiratory System

It is the pathway through which the oxygen is absorbed into the body with the help of the lungs. The respiratory system also helps in removing carbon dioxide.

Skeletal System

The Skeletal system involves bones that help in maintaining the structure of the body and provides the organs in the body with protective armor.

Each organ system undergoes a series of biological processes to have the needed effect inside our bodies. The digestive system is one of our main focuses throughout this book, as it is directly involved in the nutritional intake of our bodies. Now that we know what types of organ systems are present inside our bodies let us delve into the biological processes.

Biological Processes

These are processes that are vital for keeping an organism alive. The word 'bio' itself means 'life,' and the word 'logos' means 'information.' Biology is the information of life. The biological processes that take place inside our bodies help maintain our lives. Every human being is composed of minute particles known as 'cells.' Cells are also the basic unit of life, as every biological process involves a role played by these cells. Without cells, our bodies would not function as they do.

There are different types of cells spread throughout our bodies and are present near the organs to help them perform bodily functions. Each type of cell is specific to the function they perform. For example, the blood cells have a variety of their own types. The red blood cells help in transporting oxygen, whereas the white blood cells are involved in helping the immune system function properly, and even the plasma cells help in the clotting of blood. These cells together make up the circulatory system in the body. Similarly, every organ system has a specific set of cells that help in performing that function in the body.

The biological processes are made up of a lot of chemical reactions and other events that result in chemical transformation inside our bodies.

Metabolism

Metabolism is one of the most important biological processes inside of our bodies. The system involves a series of chemical reactions in the body that transform food into energy with the help of cells present inside our bodies. We need food to provide energy to our bodies. Without energy, we will not be able to perform tasks such as moving, thinking, and growing.

There are specific proteins that control the chemical reaction of metabolism. Proteins are macromolecules formed by amino acids. These amino acids are attached to each other in long chains to form proteins. These macronutrients are essential for building muscle mass. The process of metabolism involves breaking the food we eat into energy with the help of enzymes that are present inside our bodies. Enzymes are substances produced by an organism that catalyze (speed-up) the biochemical reactions. Three essential steps are involved during the process of metabolism:

1) Proteins are broken down into amino acids.
2) Fats are broken down into fatty acids.
3) Carbohydrates are converted into simple sugars such as glucose and fructose.

These three components are essential for providing energy to the body. These compounds are broken down and absorbed into the blood that carries it to the cells. Once these components reach the cells, other enzymes act on these broken components to speed up the chemical reaction in our body.

Anabolism

Anabolism is also known as constructive metabolism in which the proteins, fats, and carbohydrates are built and restored in the body. It involves the growth of new cells, helps in maintaining body tissue, and stores the proteins, fats, and carbohydrates for future purposes.

Catabolism

Catabolism is a destructive metabolism that breaks down larger molecules to release energy. The bonds that hold the large molecules are broken down and, as a result, these broken bonds release energy to the body.

Ketosis

Ketosis is another type of metabolic process in which body cells use up the stored fat and glucose as the first form of energy. Glucose is derived from dietary carbohydrates such as sugar and starch-containing food such as bread or pasta. These simple sugars are broken down in the body into simple sugars. Glucose is an important component that can be stored into the liver or muscles in an inactive form known as glycogen.

The body adapts to alternative strategies to meet the need for energy in the body. When the need arises, the glycogen is released in an active form of glucose, and ketones are formed as a by-product. Ketones are a derivative of organic (carboxylic) acids that are formed in the blood as a result of ketosis. Ketones are released from the body in the form of urine. Small levels of ketones help in breaking down fat;

however, a large number of ketones can poison the body. This process is known as ketoacidosis. The metabolism process can help us understand why it is crucial for our bodies to have some intake of fats, carbohydrates, and proteins in our bodies. Depriving these three resources of energy can have diverse effects on our bodies. New diets that have been formed often advise newcomers to cut down their food intake. Sadly, most of these diets constrict or forbid intake of carbohydrates entirely, and that can cause more damage to your health than you know.

As ketosis breaks down the stored fat present within the body, many diets aim to create such a metabolic state to facilitate weight loss. The diets are known as 'Keto diet' or 'Low-Carbs diet.' It is a high-fat diet in which 75% of calories are derived from fats.[1] Although this form of diet accelerates weight-loss, the end results are only temporary, and an individual faces a number of consequences when following a keto diet in the long run. It creates nutrient deficiency and can lead to diabetes-1 as it increases the number of ketones in the body. Moreover, it can lead to

---

[1] https://www.medicalnewstoday.com/articles/180858.php

ketoacidosis as well. For more detailed information, don't forget to check out myketoblog.net. The world of diet is vast and has many side-effects. Every other book published on various platforms informs us about the benefits of following a certain type of diet. Very rarely do we see the adversaries of that diet written in the book as a precaution. This book will provide you with the pros and cons of following Autophagy Diet along with clear evidence.

We all want to have a healthy body, but very rarely do we take the first step in obtaining it. It takes more willpower than one can imagine taking the first step to lose weight. Losing weight is not all about looking good – that is just one of the perks that come with it. All it takes is will-power to overpower yourself with an urge to adopt a healthier lifestyle.

Everyone wants a quick way to lose weight, but it is crucial to remember that you did not gain this weight all in one day. It will not take one day to shed this weight. Our weights are built up over the year, and it is critical that we shed weight at the same pace we gain it to be provided with long-term results. There are many people who follow various forms of diets for a shorter period of time to generate quick results. Such people mostly fall back into their bad eating habits once they get off their diets. The only way to prevent such a process of getting into a diet and losing interest in it is to completely adopt a newer lifestyle. Losing weight is all about developing a healthier lifestyle and changing your habits. Autophagy diet not only helps you in losing weight, but it also helps in creating a healthier body from inside out.

It helps the anti-aging process, forms more cells inside the body, excretes the damaged and useless cells from the body, and has a long-term effect inside your body. This form of diet has a direct impact on the body systems that can produce an effective way of losing weight.

A lot of people have yet to learn what an autophagy diet really is. It is not just another new 'trendy diet.' It involves the process of adapting practices that can completely transform our lives for the better.

Chapter 2
Autophagy – Eat Thyself, Sustain Thyself!

Have you been killing yourself every day on the treadmill, running for hours, trying to lose some pounds, but all that you end up losing by the end of the day is hope?

Every day, we walk the extra mile – quite literally – skip a meal or spend an additional hour at the gym trying to get that perfect body. Why does it not work? Is our 'healthy eating' plan too good to be true? If you want to learn more about healthy eating, check out healthyeatingadvice.com for some great advice and tips.

The reason we don't see the desired results is because of the red flags, which we only spot in hindsight. Looking back, we see them stretching all the way between us and our goals.

What can we do to achieve the milestones we want? Well, all that we need to do is channel our efforts in a way that is effective and result-oriented. Let's forget about the juice cleanses and the tasteless smoothies made in the name of detoxifiers (which probably takes months before we could feel the results). There is nothing wrong with drinking our weight in liquid kale, but it won't flush out the toxins at the pace we want it to. There's still a way not known by many that we can use to redirect our body toward self–cleansing. All we need to do is practice a little self–cannibalism. How about devouring ourselves to reduce the mass?

We can put our body on the track of eating itself. The process is known as autophagy.

The term 'Autophagy' is a compound word; its origins can be traced to ancient Greek. However, the term was officially coined by a Belgian Biochemist named Christian de Duve in 1963. It is only recently that people have begun to understand this process. 'Auto' means self, and 'phagy' translates as 'eat' or 'devour.' Thus, the literal meaning of the word 'autophagy' is 'self-eating.'

Autophagy is the body's mechanism of cleaning out damaged cells to activate the process of regeneration of new cells – newer, healthier, and better cells, to be specific. Autophagy is sometimes also referred to as 'self-devouring.' While this does not sound like something we would ever want to happen to our body, it is actually very beneficial for our overall health condition.

For starters, the basic mechanism that underlies the process of autophagy is the absence of an external source of food. In the absence of food, the body cannot develop its own food, so it eats itself. It does that by recycling and destroying the damaged cells, exploiting them by breaking into bits and proteins. This creates space for the generation of new, healthier versions of the cells to be built. Autophagy is a viable process for protecting us against lethal diseases like dementia and cancer, among others.

Autophagy can also be called an adaptive response to starvation or intermittent fasting. The process of longevity and optimal health maintenance begins when we stop eating. Thus, most of the theories suggest that intermittent fasting is one of the best ways to activate autophagy.

How Does Autophagy Works?

Let's dive into the details of how our body behaves in response to the autophagy process and what is expected from it. Over time, as our bodies and immune systems grow by age, our cells accumulate a variety of dead organelles, oxidized particles, and damaged proteins that disrupt our internal processes. This clogging acts as a catalyst for the aging process. Other catastrophic consequences are induced dementia and increased risk of a heart attack leading to other age-related diseases. These diseases are not a consequence of getting on in age, but they are a result of a growing blockage in our bodies.

The cells in our bodies, just like the ones in our brains, need to last through our lifetime. So the human body has developed a unique mechanism of ridding itself of toxic material and naturally defending itself against diseases. The process is autophagy.

Let's discuss an analogy that Naomi Whittle describes in comparison to the working mechanism of autophagy. She suggests thinking of our body as a kitchen. After preparing a meal, you clean up the kitchen counter, do the dishes, and recycle some food for the next day. Then, you take a fresh start, and you have a clean kitchen. The process of autophagy works in the same manner for your body, and it is doing a good job.

Now think of the same scenario, but this time let's consider the effects of age. You are now older and not as efficient. After preparing the meal, you leave some of it on the counter. Some of it goes into the trash can, but some of it remains forgotten in the corners or on the floor. It just sits there and rots, releasing toxic fumes. The toxic waste that has built up in your kitchen causes fermentation, releasing many toxic smells, making it unbearable to walk into the kitchen without cleaning it up. Because of the onslaught of toxins and pollutants, it becomes hard cleaning up the daily grime. The parallel drawn here is meant to show that autophagy isn't working the way it should.

Autophagy usually kicks into high gear during times of stress, to protect the body (such as in times of famine). When we activate autophagy, it slows down the aging process in the most natural way possible. It reduces inflammation in the body and boosts our overall natural ability to function properly. It helps our body develop a defensive shield against diseases and boost longevity. Once established, we can increase our autophagy response naturally with time.

The Science behind Autophagy

Let's take autophagy to the next step and discuss it in light of medical science. Over time, humans have evolved to live longer because of our ability to respond better and adequately to biological stressors. A study conducted by the University of Newcastle on a similar topic established that this ability is because of small adaptations in a protein known as p62 – the protein that induces autophagy.

By sensing metabolic byproducts that cause cell damage (known as reactive oxygen species ROS), protein p62 induces autophagy, or in simpler words, starts cleaning.

P62 Proteins removes all the toxins that your body is sheltering and equips you to better handle biological stress. The results then keep you young and healthy.

Types of autophagy

There are several types of autophagy processes. These are:

- Micro-autophagy – In this process, the cytosolic components are engulfed by the lysosomes itself through the lysosomal membrane.

- Macroautophagy – This involves the delivery of cytoplasmic cargo to the lysosome through a double membrane-bound vesicle. We call this an autophagosome that fuses with the lysosome to form an auto-lysosome.

- Chaperone-mediated autophagy – In this process, the targeted proteins translocate across the lysosomal membrane in a complex with chaperone proteins (such as Hsc-70).

- Micro and macropexophagy

- Piecemeal microautophagy of the nucleus

- Cytoplasm-to-vacuole targeting (Cvt) pathway[2]

Autophagy Helps You Maintain Homeostasis

Another benefit of autophagy is that it speeds up the process of P62 Protein, which connects directly to Homeostasis (balanced cellular function) and vibrant health. But how can we benefit from autophagy?

Benefits of Autophagy

---

[2] News Medical Life Science - https://www.news-medical.net/life-sciences/What-is-Autophagy.aspx

On a very basic level, autophagy plays a crucial part in cell functioning. It disassembles the "unnecessary or dysfunctional" cell components – the cells that might otherwise contribute to illness. Other benefits are:

- The activation of autophagy slows down the aging process.
- It prevents and/or delays neurodegenerative diseases.
- It helps reduce inflammation and bloating.
- Autophagy helps our skin. It gives our skin a healthy glow, improves complexion, and reduces acne and spots.
- Autophagy boosts our body's natural ability to function.
- Many studies have proved autophagy is a warrior against infectious disease. It regulates inflammation and bolsters the immune system.
- The lack of autophagy or autophagy deficiency has also been linked with diseases like schizophrenia and depression.
- Increased longevity is one of the many positive results of increased autophagy.
- Autophagy recycles residual proteins.

- It increases energy and helps develop cells that could benefit from potential repair.
- On a bigger scale, autophagy prompts regeneration and creates healthy cells.

Diet Changes to Boost Autophagy

Remember what we said about autophagy as literally meaning "self-eating" in the beginning? Considering that, intermittent fasting and a ketogenic diet are the best-known procedures to induce autophagy.

Eat a high fat and a low-carb diet or a keto diet. Ketosis, as we have already discussed, is a diet enriched in fats and low in carbs. It brings about the same benefits as fasting, but without fasting. It is one way of triggering autophagy with beneficial metabolic changes. A 16 to 26 hour fast helps remove the built-up toxins in the body.

The shift in caloric source provokes our body to shift its metabolic pathways. Our body needs fuel to run – that fuel is the food that we consume every day. Now, when we break the elements of food that we eat, we find vitamins, carbohydrates, proteins. All of them are necessary but in different proportions. In your keto diet, you gain 75% of our calorie intake from the fat in our food, and the rest 5 to 10% of your calories from carbs. When your body does not receive carbs, it uses fat for fuel instead of the glucose derived from carbohydrates. This begins a process of ketone production within our bodies that has many protective effects. Studies suggest that ketosis can also cause starvation-induced autophagy that has neuroprotective functions.

It activates the survival repairing mode in the body when it is on a low-sugar diet through fasting and ketosis. It brings about positive stress that wakes up the survival mode. myketoblog.net

Effects of Autophagy

Once or twice a week, we should limit our protein intake to 15-30 grams per day. This will give our body a full day to recycle the proteins. Recycling proteins helps reduce inflammation and cleanse it, causing no muscle loss.

By practicing intermittent fasting, we can increase our body's inherent autophagy process with the help of this simple pattern. Consume all our meals in 6 hours in a day, and that's it—nothing before or after that. Similar to protein-specific fasts, intermittent fasting gives our body the chance to "catch up" on all those lingering toxins — by cleaning up in real-time.

We can boost the process of autophagy by doing high-intensity interval training, better known as HIIT. It is about getting that acute stress in the short term through weight-lifting, which is one way to trigger autophagy.

Last but not least, get restorative sleep. We can burn calories even when we are asleep.

How soon do we see the results?

Autophagy provides long-term benefits to the human body, such as prevention from chronic diseases and anti-aging (or slow aging). However, it has some instant effects as well, such as weight loss. You should see the benefits of autophagy within two weeks of starting the process.

Chapter 3
Fasting

"Health and healing will follow fasting."

-Jentezen Franklin

Fasting, in its simplest form, is voluntarily giving up on food and drink for particular periods. It is also a medical therapy for several conditions and a spiritual practice in many religions, as well.

Fasting is one of the earliest therapies in medicine; it has been practiced for over a thousand years now. It originates from the oldest healing systems that recommended fasting for healing and prevention. In their writings, many doctors from ancient times have declared fasting as one of the most effective ways to boost up our health system.

The father of Western medicine, Hippocrates, believed that fasting was the ultimate way to allow our body to heal itself. Around 500 years ago, Paracelsus, yet another great name in the history of western medicine, wrote, "Fasting is the greatest remedy, the physician within." And Ayurvedic medicine, the world's oldest healing system, has long advocated fasting as a significant treatment. Fasting has roots in the different religions across the world, including Buddhism, Islam, Christianity, Judaism, as well as Hinduism. Many great religious leaders in history fasted for mental and spiritual clarity, including Buddha, Jesus, and Mohammad. In more recent history, Mahatma Gandhi led one of the most famous political acts of the previous century when he fasted for almost 21 days to promote peace.

In Europe, fasting has been used as a medical remedy for many years. Many treatment centers and spas, particularly those in Russia, Germany, and Sweden, use medically supervised fasting. In recent years in America, fasting has gained prominence as an alternative to medicinal procedures.

Fasting is a central therapy for detoxification, which is a healing method centered on the principles that illnesses and many prolonged diseases occur because of the accumulation of toxic substances in the body. The fundamental law that fasting follows is straightforward. By temporarily halting food intake, it allows our bodies a break from the continuous process of breaking down food particles into enzymes and producing chemical energy. That extra time for the body gives it a boost and the chance to replenish, heal, and restore itself. Fasting also burns the previously-stored calories (which by then become fat tissues), which work as a catalyst to remove the stored toxic substances in our body.

Our digestive tract is an organ most exposed to environmental threats, including harmful bacteria, contagious viruses, parasites, and toxins. And so, it requires the support of the immune system the most. After being broken down into small particles in the intestines, food travels through our blood to the liver, which is the largest organ of the human body's natural detoxification system.

The liver furthers the process by breaking it down and filtering out the toxic by-products released during digestion. It includes both toxins – the natural ones, and the chemical ones present in the chemically processed foods we consume. During fasting, the liver and immune system are essentially liberated to detoxify and heal other parts of the body.

How Fasting Affects Our Body

Most fasts are observed between periods of 14 and 72 hours. Intermittent fasting involves cycling between periods of fasting and eating, ranging from a few hours to a few days at a time. Also, fasting has several health benefits. From quick weight loss to better brain functioning and improved gut health, fasting is a step toward better health.

Whether you are just starting your intermittent fasting journey or you have experimented with it previously (but couldn't continue it), this chapter will help you get back on the track. Below are some health benefits of fasting:

- Fasting delays aging and extends longevity.

- It works as a catalyst in the process of weight loss. It limits calorie intake and boosts the immune system.

- According to some researchers, fasting can help in cancer prevention and increased efficiency of chemotherapy.

- It reduces insulin resistance, which promotes blood sugar control (stability).

- It improves heart health by minimizing the risks of cardiac-related conditions. It helps to control the heart rate, blood pressure levels, Triglycerides, and Cholesterol levels.

- It helps fight inflammation and hence, promotes better health.

- It prevents neurodegenerative disorders and boosts brain functioning.

- It promotes a better night's sleep.

- Intermittent fasting increases human growth hormone. This helps with fat loss and also keeps the skin looking young.

- It helps in weight loss but without the loss of muscle.

Different Types of Fasting

Though the popularity of fasting has surged in recent years, the practice dates back to centuries. Fasting played a prominent role in several ancient religions and cultures. Fasting is defined as abstinence from all or some foods or drinks for a set period. However, there are many different ways to fast.

If fasting is just about skipping food and drinks for a specific period, then why are there different types of fasting? Well, this is the most frequently asked questions that people ask before proceeding with any kind of fasting. We need to realize that with every type of food limitation, there is a different chemical reaction that takes place within our bodies. Although they all have some mutual benefits, they also possess distinctive health benefits as well that targets specific triggers.

Before we delve into finding out more about the different types of fasting, let's look at some basic types of fasting techniques:

1. **Normal Fast:** It permits drinks and food, but only allows water to be consumed.

2. **Partial Fast:** This fast allows the consumption of water, juices, or sometimes even fruit.

3. **Absolute Fast:** Neither water nor food consumption is allowed for a specific period.

These are some basic types of fast common from both scientific and religious points of view. Now, let's get into the details of different fasting techniques that are practiced globally because of the widespread awareness regarding health betterment.

Occasional Short Fasting

Whether it is about denying ourselves food, water, or other pleasures, occasional short fasting may last up to 6, 12, or even 24 hours. This makes this type of fasts very manageable. This is not a commitment, and so it is not mandatory to repeat the process. It is a short break for the body that works for many people trying to look for a start.

Extended Fasts

The beginners may find extended fasting a bit difficult than the other types of fasting. Beginning from small fasts and gaining enough resistance can help beginners prepare for extended fasts. Extended fasts last from 12 to 24 hours.

Skipping a Meal

Skipping a meal is an enhanced form of occasional short fasting. For beginners with no prior experience with intermittent fasting, but who are looking for a start, this is the easiest area that they can master.

Intermittent Fasting

Intermittent fasting is a repeated habit or repeated practice of fasting. This is a regular act of abstinence for a day a week. This type of fasting is a way of integrating the spiritual discipline of fasting into your life actively. According to its definition, intermittent fasting is fast for a prolonged period (with no food).

The thumb rule applied for intermittent fasting is the 16/8 ratio, which means we fast for 16 hours and keep the window open for the remaining 8 hours. This does not mean we can eat periodically choosing any random 8 hours a day. The 8 hours should be a consecutive period in a day.

This could be achieved by skipping a meal (breakfast, lunch, or dinner) with similar benefits. We can try skipping a meal and see if we can operate on the 16/8 ratio. The results will be visible on our body within just two weeks.

Fasting with Some Slack

We can also refer to it as fasting with a daily window. Like the 16/8 method, there are other eating windows (feeding windows) we can experiment with.

Let's face it — we are already doing this to some extent because we fast every day between dinner and breakfast the next day.

Here's what it looks like:

If we eat breakfast at 9 a.m. and our last meal of the day at 6 p.m., we eat within a 9-hour window. Therefore, we will fast for the remaining 15 hours of the day.

The next logical step to intentional intermittent fasting is widening your fasting window and narrowing your feeding window. We can try the 16/8 method, which might look something like eating all of our meals between 10 a.m. and 6 p.m.

Another example is the 18/6 method. With this one, we are raising our fasting window to 18 hours, which means eating between noon and 6 p.m.

This is a great place to start if we are serious about availing fasting benefits. It's also super easy to adapt to our unique schedule and lifestyle.[3]

Alternate Day Fasting

---

[3] https://perfectketo.com/types-intermittent-fasting/

As the name says, alternate day fasting is when we fast one complete day, then normally eat the next day and repeat the process. It can look something like this:

Monday: Fasting

Tuesday: Eating

Wednesday: Fasting

Thursday: Eating

Friday: Fasting

Saturday: Eating

Sunday: Fasting

According to the science available on alternate day fasting, we can take one of two approaches:

The first option is to fast on fasting days, only consuming water or juice. We can eat small meals up to 25% of our regular caloric intake. This equals about 500-600 calories for the average person. There's a catch, though — we shouldn't include sugar or starches in this 25%.

The second option includes "fasting-mimicking." A study suggests that this technique can help with weight loss and support heart health, too. Alternate day fasting is one of the extreme approaches of fasting and can be tough for some people to keep up with. However, if we eat nothing at all on our fasting days, the more natural way to incorporate this diet will be by limiting our fasts to not over two days a week.

Fat Fasting

Similar to ketosis or a starter for ketosis, fat fasting is an excellent way for those looking to get into ketosis quickly to lose some pounds. We can also opt for this fasting method if we are already on the weight loss plateau.

Here's a little tip: We can fat fast for 2 to 4 days, but not extend it for over five days.

Here's a little process that goes behind your skin walls and the internal digestive system. We consume 80-90 percent of our calories from just fat for 2 to 4 days. The key here is to reduce the amount of caloric intake to up to 1000-1200 calories a day only. We must remember that this type of fasting involves no open windows for any kind of cheating – sticking to the plan is essential.

This may sound easier than a complete food ban for entire days, but it still is a challenge. If you can imagine yourself eating avocadoes or cocoa butter and bullet teas/coffees for days, then this might be just the thing for you.

myketoblog.net

The Warrior Diet

The Warrior Diet, started by the former member of Israeli Special Forces Ori Hofmekler, mimics the diet plan of the ancient warriors.

As a presumable fact, these warriors kept their minds sharp and their waists slim by consuming only a small portion of a meal during a day. They consumed one big meal at night while fasting for the rest of the time.

In relation to the ketogenic diet, if we choose to eat a big meal at night, we need to ensure it is low in calories and carbs. For more on different types of diet, visit healthyeatingadvice.com

The 5:2 Ration

This diet is like a 24-hour fast and the alternate day fast in which we abstain from eating for 24 hours. But this one is quite convenient because we only need to fast twice a week for the whole day and we eat normally for the rest of the five days.

What To Eat And What To Say Goodbye To?

We need to be informed about the food we consume when fasting since we need to maintain the calorie count somewhere between 500 to 8000 calories. Thus, consume foods high in proteins, fibers, and satiation that keep us full for a longer time, so we don't feel hungry a short while after a meal. Because of this, we won't experience that dreaded sugar crush and empty-stomach feeling. Also, we need to make sure we cut on added sugars and foods high in carbs and fat (if we are not doing ketosis).

Some foods and beverages to stay away from while we fast include:

High-carbohydrate foods – Steer clear of foods such as pizza, pasta, rice, white bread, etc. If we consume these, it will cause a fluctuation of sugar levels, which will surge after the period of not consuming any food. Also, this will negate the core benefits of fasting, such as fat loss and increased insulin sensitivity.

Refined sugar – Any food that contains refined sugar in it (even honey and maple syrup) shouldn't be consumed carelessly.

Soda – This includes diet sodas, regulars, packed juices with artificial flavorings and sweeteners, sports drinks, etc. Pass up on them as they can send the benefits of fasting down the drain in no time.

Junk food and processed food – Snacks such as butter-flavored popcorn, candies, pretzels, chips, etc. should be avoided. Instead of these, we can switch to whole, natural, and preferably unpackaged foods on our fasting days.

Dairy – Do not include dairy or dairy products in your diet. Though we might be tempted to use 'low-fat' dairy products, they are not a good choice either.

So What Can We Eat?

Veggies – They are the healthiest and most nutritious food group out there. We can include as many greens in our regular meals as possible, such as spinach, broccoli, kale, and Brussels sprouts. These are high in fiber, which aids in digestion.

Fruits and Berries – While they are a good source of healthy minerals, we cannot consider eating them as freebies. These also contain calories that add up to our daily intake. We can add berries and nuts to our salads, as they are high in antioxidant levels. Nuts – They contain healthy fats, and as we already know, they are high in antioxidants. But we need to limit our intake of nuts as well, as they are high in calories.

Beans and Legumes – These include peas, beans, chickpeas, grans, and lentils, which are an excellent source of energy and protein.

High-Protein Foods – Eggs, seafood, chicken, and lean beef are all good sources of protein. They help us gain muscles and boost metabolism. Another great option is bone broth, which is known for its high nutritional value and also helps fight food cravings.

Seafood – Packed with healthy nutrients essential for the human body, especially omega–3 fatty acids, seafood is the right diet choice. Some nutrient-rich options are salmon, trout, shrimps, etc.

Whole Grains – They are a good source of protein that is also rich in fiber and low in calories.

Healthy fats – Switching to olive oil or coconut oil is suggested for optimum results in our diet.

We can consume more water – up to at least 2 liters a day. Including some healthy low-calorie beverage in our diet, either green tea, herbal tea, ginger tea, chamomile tea, is also recommended.

Fasting is the easiest way to boost our metabolism and speed up the recovery process in our bodies. It may be a little difficult initially, but has innumerable benefits that we can reap daily!

Chapter 4
Effects of Fasting

Picking up from the previous chapter, let's discuss fasting and its impact on human health.

What is fasting? Is it just a restriction on consuming food sources as fuel or energy to run your body? Or does it have more significance than that?

Fasting shows several health benefits ranging from weight loss to improved brain functioning. Fasting entails a lot of short term and long-term health benefits. In fact, if we talk about intermittent fasting, its effects are visible in a very short span – as short as a day!

Fasting today enjoys the limelight and is featured in many 'health magazines.' You can say there has been a surge in its popularity. But fasting is not something that was discovered a few years or even a few decades back. It is as ancient as human civilization. It dates back centuries, still plays a vital role in many cultures, and is a central part of most religions.

Fasting is defined as complete or partial abstinence from food and water consumption for a set period. However, there are many ways you can fast. People fast from 12 hours a day to 72 hours. In contrast to that, intermittent fasting involves a rotational shift between intervals of fasting and eating, which can range from a few hours a day to a few days a week.

The Science of Fasting

Because of the rising number of studies and research carried out on the subject, a large body of evidence now supports the benefits of fasting. The scientific process that takes place inside our bodies because of fasting cleanses it of toxins and forces cells into processes not usually simulated under a steady stream of fuel from food.

When we fast, the body does not receive its regular intake of glucose, which it usually does on routine days. This forces cells to resort to other means and materials to produce energy. The body produces gluconeogenesis - the natural process of creating its own sugar. The liver converts noncarbohydrate elements such as amino acids, lactate, and fats into glucose energy. Because of the natural process of our bodies conserving energy during fasting, our basal metabolic rate (energy burned during resting hours) becomes more efficient, which helps to balance our heart rate and blood pressure. Some elongated fast cycles (not durations, but cycles) also move a level up and result in ketosis – a process that occurs in a quick cycle. When you do not provide your body enough fats and carbs to run on, it switches its channel of energy source and starts running on stored fats instead. This creates an ideal model for weight loss and helps maintain blood sugar levels.

Fasting also puts the body under mild stress, which pushes our cells to get on track by adapting to the need; it enhances its ability to cope up. In simpler words, the cells become stronger than they were before. They become more resilient and resistant to diseases.

This process is similar to what occurs when we put our bodies under strict physical training regimes. We stress our cardiovascular systems during workouts, and it helps us gain physical strength. One reason most people recommend short-term fasting instead of longing durations of fasts is because of the body's requirement to restore and replenish. Even with physical exercise, you can only develop muscle when you let your body rest and recover. Fasting is like that, too, only you are putting not just your body but also your metabolism under stress.

Fasting and Its Impact

It sounds so simple, doesn't it? No cooking, no keeping the calorie count, no choices. Just say 'no' to food, and your fasting starts! You get on track with quick weight loss and other health benefits as soon as you step on the road to fasting.

Since fasting, especially intermittent fasting, has gained a lot of popularity around the globe, many celebrities are doing it too. Some of them are also known for inventing their customized diets, which involve fasting intervals and healthy eating to influence their physical and mental health. One such example is of Beyoncé, a famous American singer and celebrity who lost 20 pounds of her total body weight just by fasting.

But what about the rest of us? Will it work the same for us? Is fasting an actual way of losing weight effectively? Would it help us achieve greater longevity? Can fasting be a useful tool to treat severe medical conditions such as rising cholesterol, blood sugar, and blood pressure levels? Does fasting help in asthma, arthritis, and other such auto-immune disorders? Well, it sure does – if not entirely, then to a noticeable extent. If it didn't have all those benefits, not all religions would share the ideology of fasting! Muslims recognize the holy month of Ramadan as a month of fasting. Catholics fast on Ash Wednesday and Good Fridays. Yom Kippur is a renowned event where Jews observe six days of fasting. Hindus fast in a similar fashion during the full moon and for other congregational prayers. Mormons observe a fast on every first Sunday of each month. And that's not it. Followers of other beliefs, such as Buddhism and Jainism, also have their fasting routines.

Many of these religions practice fasting because of the belief that it connects them to their spiritual being – that is, it becomes a connection between the physical and spiritual state. However, in the modern era, fasting is not limited to spiritual guidance anymore. Instead, it is seen as a health booster.

Fasting and Weight Loss

As we walk through all the controversy about fasting and weight loss, we discover that most medical experts and researchers agree that fasting has many benefits besides just weight loss. It is one of the quickest, easiest, and cheapest methods of losing some pounds. Usually, the food you consume in a day burns up to provide energy (fuel) to run your body. The body uses only as much food as it needs to run our system properly throughout the day, and it stores the excess amount. Instead of getting used up as a fuel, it is stored in the form of body fats for future use. Weight gain occurs when the stored food never gets used as we consume another meal.

When we fast, we stop consuming food, which pushes our body to reconvert the stored fats and use them as an energy source. We know this process as lipolysis. An edge that fasting has is the burning the fat cells – the process is faster through fasting than any other diet. Also, the fat burned during fasting does not result in loss of muscle mass, which is a primary concern for most men with workout routines. Therefore, through fasting, athletes manage to reduce body fat percentage before competitions.

Fasting brings a change in our lifestyle. It makes it more effective and sustainable compared to crash dieting courses and weight loss supplements. Most studies have found fasting to be one of the most healthy, reliable, and durable solutions for weight loss and body-mass maintenance.

Fasting and Metabolism

Fasting helps boost metabolism!

Our ability to burn fat and metabolize food is affected because of our weak metabolism. Our body receives some rest to recover when we perform intermittent fasting, which gives some time to our digestive tract to relax.

When we eat after the rest, our metabolism is boosted, and that enables our body to burn calories more efficiently and extract greater energy from the food that we consume. This is one reason it is one of the safest weight loss methods.

Department of Internal Medicine IV conducted a study at the University of Vienna regarding fasting and its impact. The study yielded results in favor of fasting, proving it to be one way to increase our metabolism by up to 14%.

Another study discovered that fasting acts as a catalyst, leading to a fast increase in the levels of the neurotransmitter norepinephrine in our bloodstream. This further contributes to increased metabolism. Intermittent fasting also leads to healthy bowel function.

"Recent Aging studies have shown that caloric restriction and fasting have a prolonging effect on lifespan in model animals."

-Dr. Takayuki Teruya

Fasting and Blood Glucose

Because of increased rates of obesity and sedentary lifestyles of people, the world faces many health issues problems. For instance, in the past two decades, the number of people who have Type 2 diabetes has climbed to alarming levels. This condition is characterized by a reduced level of insulin sensitivity, which results in increased blood sugar levels.

Typically, when we eat, the food is broken down into particles. This broken-down food leads to a surge in sugar levels in your blood. However, to meet the requirement of the body, the pancreas produces its own insulin, which triggers glucose absorption (blood sugar) from the blood by fat and muscle cells – which then use this glucose as a source of energy. This process helps reduce blood sugar levels to the healthy, acceptable range. Sometimes when the body's normal sensitivity to insulin drops, the body requires more and more insulin to help regulate sugar levels in the bloodstream. When this happens, the pancreatic cells are worn out by the end because of the high demand.

Eventually, the body gives up on producing enough insulin to maintain healthy sugar levels in your blood. This leads to a drastic drop and a surge in blood sugar levels, which eventually leads to type 2 diabetes.

People often take an external medicated form of insulin to boost their health system. But let's be real, this medicine is expensive; it is not readily available, and not everyone can afford it.

Another alternative (not a substitute) for increasing insulin sensitivity for people with insulin resistance is intermittent fasting. When we fast, the body uses the glucose within the bloodstream and the liver, since there is no other external source of sugar available. This helps to lower blood sugar levels.

Besides that, once you break your fast, your insulin becomes more effective at absorbing glucose by the muscle and the fat cells. Most of the stored glucose (excess) in your body would have already been used up. Your pancreas also stops producing insulin and no longer goes under stress, since your body needs no more insulin at this point. This eventually leads to less stress on the inner system of the body and low levels of insulin requirement. This results in lower risks of developing type 2 diabetes and better overall health.

Several studies show the effectiveness of fasting on insulin sensitivity. One such study carried out by the team of experts from the University of Illinois found that fasting results in the decrease of insulin levels for up to 20 to 32%. It also reduces the blood sugar level by 3 to 6%. Another study established that fasting can also help prevent severe kidney damage, which may result from diabetes. All this points to the conclusion that fasting can help prevent Type–2 Diabetes. Scientists believe that intermittent fasting plays an integral role in the management of Type–2 Diabetes.

The benefits of fasting are hard to ignore. The results might be slow but are definitely long-term. To avail yourself of the best results of fasting, you must fast once or twice a week for your body to get in a healthy fasting routine.

Chapter 5
The Science Behind Autophagy

In the previous chapter, we discussed the overtime response of the human body. As our bodies and immune systems grow by age, our cells accumulate a variety of dead organelles, oxidized particles, and damaged proteins that disrupt our internal processes. This fuels the aging process, and then, further consequences induce dementia and increase the risk of a heart attack. These diseases are not a consequence of getting on in age; instead, they result from a growing blockage in our bodies.

The cells in our bodies, just like the ones in our brains, need to last through our lifetime. The human body has developed a unique mechanism of ridding itself of toxic material and naturally defending itself against diseases – autophagy. The underlying mechanism that underlies the process of autophagy is the absence of an external source of food. When the body is not fed from an external food source, it eats itself since it cannot produce its own food. It does so by recycling and destroying the damaged cells and reusing them by breaking it into proteins. This results in the regeneration of new, healthier versions of the cells in the body. Autophagy is a viable process for protecting us against lethal diseases like dementia and cancer, among others.

Autophagy is also referred to as an adaptive response to starvation or intermittent fasting. The process of longevity and optimal health maintenance begins when we stop eating. Thus, most of the theories suggest that intermittent fasting is one of the best ways to activate autophagy.

We have learned the basics of autophagy and how we can boost the process of autophagy. Previously we discussed:

- Basics of the internal system – how autophagy works?

- Types of autophagy

- Benefits of autophagy

- Effects of autophagy

- Diet changes to boost autophagy

In this chapter, we will discuss the process involved in autophagy – what does science say about this process? What is the mechanism that takes place within our bodies?

The Science Behind Self-Cannibalization

We know by now that autophagy is the process of self–cannibalization. The captured organelles and cytoplasm by the cells get consumed in the lysosomes. The resulting broken-down products work as fuel (inputs) to cellular metabolism. Through this process, the body uses these products to generate energy and build new membranes and proteins.

The damaged and outdated cellular components are replaced by fresh ones, preserving the health of cells and tissues in the autophagy process. Autophagy provides an internal source of energy through nutrients in the absence of external food supply. Autophagy prevents degenerative diseases and is a powerful booster of metabolic homeostasis as well.

In literal terms, autophagy translates to self-eating and is one significant way your body detoxifies. In autophagy, the affected cells dwindle over time by breaking into various molecules. New ones readily replace them. This process helps cells survive low-nutrient conditions.

In a series of steps, a vesicle precursor, known as the phagophore, forms; cellular content accumulates as it matures into an autophagosome. Then, after fusion with a lysosome, the inner vesicle of the autophagosome is digested along with the cargo, and the products release into the cytoplasm. Over the past 25 years, researchers have detailed the molecular regulators of this process, with recent insights highlighting autophagy's link to both health and disease.[4]

The mean span of life is regaining its extension with time as we evolve to live longer because of our improved response to biological stressors. As per a study conducted by Newcastle University recently, it is believed that the reason behind this is that of small adaptations in P63 protein, which induces autophagy.

The cleaning process or the induction of autophagy begins through activation of the P62 Protein – through sensing the metabolic byproducts that result in cell damage. The P62 Protein removes all the damaged cells and organelles that have occupied our bodies. This equips our

---

[4]https://www.the-scientist.com/infographics/infographic-how-autophagy-works-30029

body with an enhanced ability to bear biological stress. This stress management and endurance defy our body's aging process, keeping us young and healthy for more extended periods.

However, only humans possess this capacity. Lower organisms, such as fruit flies, do not adhere to this nature. A research team was set up to find more about the human protein, P62, that allows ROS sensing. As a result of several experiments, genetically modified flies were created with "humanized protein – P62." Compared to normal flies, the "humanized-protein-flies" showed a changed behavior; they survived longer in stressful conditions and bore additional stress efficiently.

The lead doctor of this study, Dr. Viktor Korolchuk, said about this experiment: "This tells us that abilities, such as sensing stress and activating protective processes like autophagy, may have evolved to allow better stress resistance and a longer lifespan."

Kick Starting Autophagy

The question you have probably never asked yourself before is: "How do I eat myself?"

It's time we tell you how!

Stress is probably one of the worst things one could be immune to. However, not all stress is bad. To activate autophagy, you may need to put your body through some hardship. Short-term difficulty can bring about long-term benefits for the body. This will fuel up the process of self-cannibalism or autophagy.

Here are the three main ways to boost autophagy in your body.

Lower, and lower and lower your carb intake!

Compared to the rest, this is one of the easiest ways to put your body on autophagy. This way, you won't have to jeopardize your rib-eye steak for the sake of good health. However, you may have to give up on the garlic bread and candied items. This is an intermediary process that puts your body on ketosis. myketoblog.net

In ketosis, we switch the fuel channel for the body by starving it of carbs. We push our bodies to consume fats to burn as a primary source of producing energy. This is the magic that goes behind a ketogenic diet. The body achieves ketosis after a certain amount of time into intermittent fasting, which is exactly what our next topic of discussion is: Fasting and Autophagy.

Autophagy and Fasting

Another stressful act, which we may not readily adopt, but from which the body receives ultimate benefits in the long-term, is fasting – that is, skipping meals! Many pieces of research have proven that the consequences of fasting are favorable. According to one study, intermittent fasting and autophagy are believed to be effective treatments to cure cancer. They also prevent normal cells from deteriorating and have very few side effects as compared to other resources.

Another study showed that intermittent fasting that leads to autophagy improves the brain's cognitive functioning, structure, and neuroplasticity – the brain's ability to rebuild and recognize itself.

Fasting (or intermittent fasting) brings about pronounced health benefits such as longevity, weight loss, and decreased risk for heart diseases and diabetes. A lot of research has been conducted to discover the optimum health benefits of fasting. Lab monkeys and mice that fast in lab experiments were observed to have a healthy lifespan and live longer than the ones regularly fed. According to the findings of the research, restricting calorie intake activates the genes which inform cells to preserve resources. The cells perform a defensive mechanism where they go into 'famine mode' or 'preservation mode.' In this phase, they become more resilient to cellular stress and diseases. And this is the stage of fasting that triggers autophagy.

We know fasting as the number one booster of activating autophagy in the human body. For instance, during the fast, if you have made it till 18 hours of skipping meals, your body switches to fat-burning mode. It generates significant ketones, pushing you into ketosis. Ketones act as signaling molecules by the time their number level increases within the body. Similar to hormones, they command your body to ramp up stress-busting pathways, which repairs damaged DNA and reduces inflammation.

Within 24 hours of fasting, your body shifts from ketosis to autophagy, where your cells increasingly recycle old compounds and particles. This process breaks down the misfolded proteins that link to severe diseases such as Alzheimer's.

Fasting is a powerful way to boost autophagy!

Because of our cells' inability to start autophagy, we can suffer from neurodegenerative diseases as well. Autophagy is an essential process for the rejuvenation of tissues and cellular organelles. Fasting helps to activate the AMPK signaling pathway and inhibits mTOR activity. This results in a boosted autophagy process. However, upon cutting the glucose storage, our insulin level drops, which is also not good for health. Thus, we must maintain balance.

Also, autophagy helps to destroy any remnants of lingering bacteria if our body has had been through an infectious disease recently.

However, keep in mind that fasting is generally not recommended for pregnant women and children. It can also be harmful to people with diabetes and other blood sugar issues. So, carry out due diligence before you decide to fast.

Autophagy without Fasting

Can we induce autophagy without fasting?

Well, the answer is yes! We can.

According to theories about the activation of autophagy, it is also possible to induce it without putting our bodies through the stress of fasting for long hours. However, the effort put into this process will be much harder. And the process will be a bit longer than it usually is with fasting.

Autophagy is a constant biological repair process occurring in our bodies. Fasting gives a slight push, creating an internal environment for the body to adapt to quick repair processes. These repairs occur across all tissues through a variety of mechanisms and other subprocesses.

Caloric restriction, along with significant resting intervals, improve autophagy cycle times, making it more efficient. However, the effects are not as fast and efficient as those induced by fasting.

There are other ways where non-fasters can induce and catalyze the process of autophagy, such as by consuming specific foods and having a consistent exercise pattern. Some additional tips to induce autophagy with no fasting are:

1. Consume more liquids and increase your average daily intake of water.

2. Drink autophagy-favorable teas that boost metabolism and speed up autophagy processes such as black coffee, green tea, ginseng tea.

3. Consume more autophagy boosting or autophagy friendly spices such as ginseng, ginger, cumin.

4. Explore better alternatives to regular foods. For instance, consuming foods that have ingredients such as mushrooms, coconut oil, pomegranates, green peas, and lentils are a good option.

5. Practice intermitting fasting. Don't get this wrong; we are still discussing how to induce autophagy without fasting. By gradually practicing intermitting fasting, we restrict not all but some excess food intake. Limiting incoming nutrients, we put it under stress and stimulate autophagy, despite the temporary nutritional dip.

6. An alternative to any type of fasting would be a ketogenic diet. By cutting off the supply of carb intake in the body, we force the body to consume fats as a primary fuel to run the body. To do so, the body is set on ketosis – a switch that helps boost autophagy. This aids not just in body fat loss but also in reducing the risk of diabetes.

7. Take rest and have some good quality sleep. Here's another reason to have an extended sleep: autophagy occurs even when we sleep. Our cells clear out the cobweb while we dream about attaining that figure we have desired for a very long time.

8. Take both cold and hot water baths. Alternate between sauna or steam room time with hot and cold showers. Both of them stress the cells and promote autophagy.

9. Add supplements to your diets to support autophagy. These include omega-3 fish oils, MCT Oil, and Vitamin D.

10. Exercise is a must, whether you fast or not. When fasting, you don't need to go overboard with exercising. However, in a non–fasting state, you may have to concentrate more on burning some calories with extensive exercising. Visit myexerciseblog.com for free videos, bodyweight exercise tips, and workout-at-home videos.

11. You can start by adding aerobics in your daily routine to get yourself pumped. Then, you may eventually increase your levels by incorporating miles walking, swimming laps, running, cycling, etc. They all stress the body in a good way and turn up the autophagy heat as well.

12. In response to the exercise, for the neurological mechanism that upregulates autophagy, there is a requirement of more extensive research. Previous studies suggested that Sirt1 levels increase by exercising. This is closely linked with insulin regulation and increased AMPK activation. AMPK itself is a protein that increases glucagon levels. Exercise may increase autophagy levels by decreasing insulin levels and, thus, growing glucagon to induce autophagy. Also, by increasing AMPK activation, it can increase glucagon levels directly.

Although there is still a lot of work to do, with topics such as fasting and autophagy under the microscope of each research facility, the bottom line here is that autophagy supports the anti-aging process and provides many other health benefits. To cultivate a healthy lifestyle, we must work on the roots. Adopt healthy behaviors such as proper sleep, a non-sedentary lifestyle, enough exercise, and eating healthy and see the benefits for yourself.

Section
Getting Ready

Chapter 6
What Can Autophagy Do For You?

We already know what autophagy is all about. It is the process where our cells can repair damage and heal themselves. Once activated, we can put this healing method to use effectively. The activation is induced when our body needs to fight an infection or repair damage or when we need to save energy.

Since autophagy gained limelight in medical research, it became a hot topic for pharma countries and the new buzzword for health town. Drug companies and academics are in a constant rush to find solutions and alternatives such as drugs that will stimulate the process, or at least catalyze it. With the race at its peak pace, nutrition companies and health and wellness authorities are also stepping on the bandwagon by coming up with new solutions that claim to be better than the previous one. Some of these solutions are viable, such as restricting carbohydrate and calorie intake, high-intensity exercise, intermittent fasting, etc.

Autophagy occurs at a low level when things are running smoothly in a cell, helping recycle worn-out cellular components and rejuvenating the other organelles. It serves as a 'maintenance' mode.

However, when things undergo stress mechanism in a cell (lacking enough energy/nutrients, dysfunctional components, or microbe's invasion), *autophagy* is induced. It implies that autophagy is a stress generated response. Our body turns it up to help us protect via a 'stress response' mode. This chapter includes details about the wide range of processes where autophagy has an impact and what it really does for us and our bodies.

There's an array of a wide range of areas shadowed by the process of autophagy and its impact. Let's dive into the details of how autophagy affects us and what it can do for us:

Autophagy and Metabolism

Autophagy is a process of recycling and rejuvenating cells in our bodies. It detoxifies our body by replacing all cell parts, such as mitochondria. Mitochondria is a part of our cell that can also be referred to as the cellular engine.

They make ATP and burn fat – your body's energetic fuel supply. However, because of the processing within a small-capacity cell part, Mitochondria builds up harsh toxic substances within itself that can damage the whole cell. The process of autophagy breaks down that toxic build-up and proactively saves future damage to our cells. This effect is not only restricted to mitochondria but extends to the rest of the cellular parts as well. By breaking down and building up cell rejuvenation, the whole cellular process works more efficiently; it not just burns fat cells but also builds proteins. The healthier the cells, the more efficient they become.

Autophagy and Neurodegenerative Diseases

The proteins in and around our brain cells misfold and don't work 'right.' So, many age-related brain diseases take a long while to develop. Autophagy helps cells get rid of the proteins that are no longer doing their jobs and are just taking up space. For instance, if we speak of Alzheimer's disease, autophagy helps to remove amyloid – an abnormal protein produced in the bone marrow and deposited in tissue or organs. Autophagy is not activated because of high blood sugar levels, making the situation difficult for the cells to clear out the clutter.

Autophagy and Sugar levels

Insulin is the hormone that allows cells to absorb glucose from the bloodstream to use later as energy.

When a surplus supply of food is available, it decreases the affectivity of insulin, making it less sensitive. This means that cells no longer actively respond to insulin signals, which leads to a higher level of glucose and fat accumulation.

However, in autophagy, when the food supply is restricted to a specific limitation, the human body tries to conserve as much as possible.

Autophagy and Inflammation

Through helping to boost the immune response needed by our body, autophagy encourages a 'goldilocks' amount of inflammation. It holds the ability to increase inflammation in the presence of an invader by triggering the immune system to attack. In contrast to that, autophagy works to reduce inflammation from our immune system by removing the signals – antigens, a form of protein – that are triggering it.

Autophagy and infectious Diseases

Autophagy helps to trigger an immune response if needed. It is responsible for removing certain microbes from the cells inside such as Mycobacterium Tuberculosis and certain viruses such as HIV.

Autophagy also helps to remove toxins caused by infections. This is especially important for food-borne illnesses.

Autophagy and Cancer Onset

Pro-cancer processes, such as chronic inflammation, DNA damage response, and genome instability can be suppressed with the aid of autophagy. As part of a study conducted by researchers on genetically engineered mice, subjects that lacked autophagy had higher risks of cancer.

However, as cancer progresses, autophagy may be activated to obtain alternative fuel. There is still a lot more research needed in this field, however.

Autophagy and Digestive Health

Since chronic immune response in the gut can overwhelm and swell our bowels, a chance to repair, rest and restore will help improve gut health. To obtain optimum benefits, we need to activate our autophagy with a schedule that allows for an extended overnight fast, so we provide our gut the space it needs to heal.

Autophagy and Skin

Our skin cells are vulnerable to external factors. These are the cells most exposed to the world. They also take a lot of damage from surrounding elements such as heat, rays, light, weather changes, pollution, chemicals, and physical damage. Our skin cells age in place when they accumulate toxins and undergo damages.

Although our body has its ways of growing back the skin cell layer, independent of the autophagy process, it still entails many benefits for our skincare. For instance, it can help repair the existing cells to bring a glow on our faces. It supports skin cells clearing the clutter out, such as engulfed bacteria that damage the body.

Autophagy and Body Weight

Autophagy supports a healthy weight. The following are some benefits of autophagy, which supports healthy weight:

• Fat burning activates autophagy, but the process spares protein. This saves us from losing muscle mass that makes up for our body shape. One might lose their muscle mass on extended fasting periods; however, with shorter fasts, we can activate autophagy. This will help us retain protein while burning fat and becoming leaner.

• Autophagy quells unnecessary inflammation in the body. Insulin levels increase because of chronic inflammation, which leads to more fat storage. Thus, reduced inflammation helps to reduce insulin levels from the bloodstream.

• Autophagy reduces toxins in our cells. As long as these toxins are being extracted, we are less likely to need fat cells to store them.

• Autophagy helps to repair cell parts responsible for making and packaging proteins. It supports metabolic efficiency by repairing such cells that process energy. This is helpful when cells are required to switch to fat-burning mode to produce energy.

Autophagy and Muscle Performance

During exercise and muscle-building, the stretches cause micro-tears and results in muscle inflammation. This calls for muscle repairing, which demands increased energy. Your muscle cells respond to this by undergoing autophagy. It reduces the requirement of energy levels for the muscle, degrades damaged components, and improves the balance of energy to mitigate future damage.

Autophagy and Apoptosis

Autophagy helps minimizes apoptosis. Apoptosis is also referred to as the programmed death of your cells. If you think the process is like that of autophagy, it's not. The cellular decay in apoptosis creates a mess to clean up, which causes our body to induce inflammation for the clean-up.

Because cells repair themselves, our bodies put lesser effort into cleaning up the old ones and developing new ones. Hence, tissue renewal involves lesser inflammation. The saved energy could build up new cells to replace the previous ones.

Autophagy and Aging

The accumulation of damaged cellular components associated with age can be counteracted by autophagy. Autophagy also enhances the metabolic efficiency of cells.

It helps build cells become more resilient since that itself is a response to stress. It also removes dysfunctional harmful mitochondria responsible for producing an abundance of harmful ROS (Reactive Oxygen Species), which degrade the cell. These processes are reported to extend the lifespan of several species in this world.

Chapter 7
Autophagy and Obesity

In the current age where technology and innovation have taken over the world, everything is continually changing. With each development, the possibilities are expanding in several dimensions. However, from another perspective, with each invention, our world is also growing smaller day by day.

The previous decades kept us tangled in wires, but with modern technology, this problem is eliminated as the world has gone wireless. Everything today is in our reach, practically a single tap away. From switching on the lights of our room to ordering groceries, electronic media devices have enslaved people. While technology has made our lives easier, the downside is that it has limited the human capacity to perform in life.

The integration of technology in all facets of our lives, from our homes to workplaces, means that we lead highly sedentary lives today. As a result, obesity is on the rise. It poses severe threats to human health and causes many diseases such as diabetes mellitus, inflammation, cancer, insulin resistance, hypertension, sleep apnea. The current focus of scientific and medical research is on limiting caloric intake. However, the efficacy of this approach remains poor. There is a vital need for understanding its pathophysiology to treat and manage obesity and its related complications. Research on the aetiological mechanism underpinning obesity has equipped us with a relative framework that emphasizes neurohormonal dysregulation and energy imbalance. Autophagy tightly regulates all these activities.

Following that, there is an emerging interest in autophagy's role in the maintenance of cellular homeostasis and organ functioning – a conserved homeostatic process for cellular quality through removal and recycling of cellular components. It is done by selectively getting rid of potentially toxic proteins, organelles, and lipids from the cells.

Excessive fat accumulation through increased body weight characterizes obesity, which is increasing at a rapid rate in all age groups today. Obesity is linked with severe metabolic disturbances and significant pathology in several organs, including the heart. Metabolic flexibility for the mitochondrial production of adenosine-5 is restricted because of excessive fat intake. This may lead to inflammation and, to some extent, cellular injury. We know this as a significant underlying cause in the pathogenesis of many diseases. For instance, lipid overload causes toxic effects and impacts cardiac functioning.

Autophagy is referred to as an evolved conserved mechanism that maintains nutrient and cellular homeostasis. This is done by disregarding the damaged organelles and misfolded proteins. Dysregulation of autophagy is found to be linked with cardiorenal metabolic syndrome, including hypertension, insulin resistance, and maladaptive immune modulation.

A recent study conducted on autophagy and its impact on the cardiac system found that autophagy plays a distinctive role in each different cell and situation. Besides that, a particular type of autophagy, known as the mitophagy, is proven essential for homeostasis of a healthy network of functional mitochondria.

Lipophagy, mitophagy, and autophagy, all are key recycling processes for protein aggregates, damaged mitochondria in adipose tissues, and excess fat. WAT (White

Adipose Tissue) hypertrophy and hyperplasia, and BTA (Brown Tissue Aplasia) are often associated with increased body weight or obesity. This contributes significantly to the lipid metabolism imbalance and free fatty acid release.

As per recent studies, obese and diabetic patients were observed to have hyperactive autophagy in WAT. Also, it required active mitochondria clearance through activation of autophagy for beige/brown fat whitening – that is, conversion to white fat. However, inhibition of autophagy seemed detrimental in hypermetabolic conditions such as hepatic steatosis, atherosclerosis, thermal injury, sepsis, and cachexia through an increase in free fatty acid and glycerol release from WAT.[5]

The emerging concept of white fat browning – conversion to beige/brown fat – has been controversial in its anti-obesity effect through the facilitation of weight loss and improving metabolic health. Therefore, proper regulation of autophagy to fit an individual metabolic profile is necessary to ensure balance in adipose tissue, metabolism, and function.

---

[5] https://www.ncbi.nlm.nih.gov/pmc/articles/PMC5596561/

Tips to Maintain Autophagy

While we know autophagy helps people lose weight, many advocates fail because they are hard to stick to.

It can take some time to adapt to an entirely new eating schedule. But keeping ourselves busy keeps our mind off food and focus on the real long-term benefits.

Someone who is really fasting drinks water and nothing else. But it's okay to bend the rules sometimes to get through long hours without food. Coffee and tea can effectively curb appetite. While black coffee is perfect, a little cream is also acceptable. The same applies to bone broth.

It all depends on our goal. If we're trying to lose weight, we can eat around 500 calories and lose weight, along with alternate-day fasts.

But most people will strictly have to stick to drinking water if they wish to achieve more benefits of fasting. The protein found in both cream and broth will shut down the autophagy process in which cells deteriorate and recycle themselves.

Key Notes!

- Along with cellular energy, glucose, amino acids, and lipid metabolism are regulated by autophagy. In contrast to that, the autophagy revolution is governed by the levels of ATP, fatty acids, amino acids, and glucose.

- In obesity owing to overnutrition or dyslipidemia, autophagy might either be suppressed or enhanced.

- The generation and development of metabolic disorders can result from autophagy dysregulation.

- Chronological biphasic changes and tissue specificity is exhibited through autophagy dysregulation throughout overnutrition.

- You may expect unfavorable effects on local or global metabolism (which promotes metabolic disorders) because of the loss of autophagy homeostasis in adipose tissue. For example, despite elevated expression of autophagy genes, adipocyte autophagy diminishes.

- For optimum results, changing the lifestyle and daily routine, incorporating a few exercises, and dietary restrictions will help. This can prevent and treat body obesity and its complications.

Remember, fasting is not just a way to lose some extra weight, but a lifestyle. Even for people who don't fast regularly, it is beneficial to do so once in a while to maintain a healthy and fit body. healthyeatingadvice.com has some great ways for you to not just devise a diet plan but also to help you stay on track.

Chapter 8
Autophagy and Anti-Aging

Proceeding with our analysis of autophagy and its effects, let's discuss the phenomenon of the aging process. We know that any process related to human health has consequences that reverberate through various aspects of human health, physical as well as mental. Similarly, autophagy has an extensive range of benefits for health, which includes anti-aging and longevity.

Fasting is a triggering molecule that can delay the aging of our artery. Research has come up with substantial evidence that supports the cure of some chronic age-related diseases, such as cardiovascular issues, cancer, and even Alzheimer's.

What is aging?

It is a gradual process during which humans undergo an exponential vitality decline, eventually leading to death. Several new kinds of research have presented findings that defy previous myths regarding human health. Who would have thought self- cannibalism would be a good thing for your body? Multiple longevity pathways and age-reversing procedures are now being discussed, such as dietary restriction, TOR signaling, and insulin-like growth factors signaling mitochondrial activity.

One prominent mention in these studies is autophagy, which shows the evolutionary conserved lysosomal degradation pathway. Autophagy revolves around the idea of regulating and keeping body cells in proper balance. We also know this as homeostasis. You must have heard the famous saying about environmental stability to "Reduce, Reuse, and Recycle." Similarly, autophagy depicts the natural paradigm of the sustainability process, i.e., breaking down cellular organisms to recycle them and produce newer, fresher cells.

Is It Necessary to Look Old As You Age?

Aging is a complex process. This biological course results in gradual decomposition of aberrant organelles and macromolecules. The accumulation of such misfolded and oxidized molecules can harm tissue and organ integrity. This can also affect cellular homeostasis negatively. Aging can also occur because of direct or indirect interventional activity of defective molecules with functional molecules (responsible for age maintenance and keeping you young). This gradual destruction leads to a further decaying process leading to aging and, ultimately, death.

However, with new research being done on the same subject, our understanding has expanded over the past couple of decades. Especially molecular intervention that causes aging is being studied and researched on a wider horizon. In many model organisms, the findings have concluded that aging can be modulated by altering pathways, changing dietary patterns, and conserved signaling. This raises the possibility of regulating the aging process through therapeutic manipulation.

As some observe in different organisms, proper maintenance of autophagic activity results in extended longevity. This chapter discusses the impact of autophagy on the activity of cells and similar age-related issues. Understanding the paradigm at which autophagy operates creates wider opportunities for the newer scientific phenomenon (both biochemical and pharmacological) to be discovered and worked upon. Such findings target the development of anti-aging potions (therapeutic approaches).

Because of autophagy, we can say that it is not necessary to look old as you advance in years. In fact, if done correctly, you can reverse the process and look younger than your actual age!

Autophagy in Aging

According to research, the relationship between autophagy augmentation and extended lifespan has been reported in exceptionally healthy centenarian humans, who have increased levels of BECLIN1, compared to young people. We hope that in the next years, these preliminary studies will be more advanced, and give us insights into the longevity mechanisms of humans from clinical case studies.

Why does the probability of cancer rise as we age? Well, this is probably because of the decline of the homeostatic process and the increased accumulation of protein aggregates and ROS (potentially considered as harmful molecules). Autophagic procedures help prevent certain age-related diseases as well, for instance, with a tumor. Autophagy serves two purposes in the tumorigenesis, one of them – the dominating one – is the suppression of tumor progression.

Caloric Restriction and Its Anti-Aging Benefits

Calorie restriction and intermittent fasting are the two most discussed and linked topics with autophagy. Let us recall some basic principles that induce and catalyze the autophagic processes.

In previous chapters, we discussed some ways to induce autophagy or some of the ways to put your body on the autophagic track. Here's a quick recap. Autophagy is a constant biological repair process occurring in our bodies. Fasting gives it a slight push, creating the right environment for the body to adapt to quick repair processes.

Caloric restriction, along with significant resting intervals, improve autophagy cycle times, making it more efficient. However, the effects are not as fast and effectual as those induced by fasting.

There are other ways where non-fasters can induce and catalyze the process of autophagy, such as by consuming specific foods and having a consistent exercise pattern. Some additional tips to induce autophagy with no fasting are:

1. High liquid consumption: Increase your average daily intake of water.

2. Autophagy-favorable teas: These are drinks that can boost metabolism. Incorporate them into your daily diet. These calorie-controlled drinks act as a catalyst for the autophagy processes. A few examples of such beverages are black coffee, green tea, ginseng tea.

3. Increase your consumption of autophagy-friendly spices such as ginseng, ginger, cumin.

4. Switch to healthy alternatives – Opt for foods with ingredients such as mushrooms, coconut oil, pomegranates, green peas, and lentils are a good option.

Besides these, it is highly recommended to practice intermitting fasting. By gradually practicing intermitting fasting, we restrict not all but some excess food intake. Limiting incoming nutrients, we put it under stress and stimulate autophagy despite the temporary nutritional dip. Another aim of intermittent fasting is to control daily caloric intake. We know caloric restriction is the most efficient method to battle the aging process.

Researches based on animals and humans have explained many previously unknown bodily mechanisms and behaviors. Of these, four of the topmost mechanisms backed by caloric restriction are mentioned below. These mechanisms underpin healthy aging and even the reverse-aging process. These include:

- Mitochondrial Physiology

- Antioxidants

- Cell Proliferation

- Inflammation

Humans have a complicated relationship with aging. What's worth noticing here is the fact that these mechanisms interrelate!

Autophagy and Longevity – the Lively Duo!

We term autophagy and longevity as the 'lively duo' because the term applies literally to the scenario. Both processes are closely linked with each other! Let's dig in further. We observe degeneration with the induction of autophagic genes in mammalian cells. This degeneration is linked with a similar process, commonly known as 'aging.' However, with age, autophagy drops down. So you can imagine the upshot of this very scientific explanation. We project on mitigating age with the stimulation of autophagy.

In the study of some age-related diseases (such as atherosclerosis), the effects of autophagy cannot be overshadowed. Atherosclerosis is a commonly occurring disease (because of high cholesterol levels and other such factors). It is characterized by the narrowing and hardening of arteries, which restricts blood flow around the body freely. This is due to the formation of plaque. Atherosclerosis, if unattended, may lead to some other serious conditions such as strokes, cardiac attacks, and other circulatory diseases.

According to one study, the formation of plaque and the constriction of arteries is linked to reduced autophagy. Scientists bred mice to achieve enhanced autophagy by increasing the expression of a gene known as TFEB. The results of the experiment were in favor of human health. The change seems to cast a shield or some protection against diseases such as atherosclerosis. Yoshinori Ohsumi laid the foundation of this scientific process. Ohsumi, a Japanese cell biologist, has contributed to modern science through his extensive research and studies. Ohsumi won a Nobel Prize in Medicine in 2016 for his research on the process of cell recycling and renewal–autophagy.

According to him, fasting is one way that activates autophagy, which helps stop the aging process and has a positive impact on overall cell renewal. Ohsumi stated: *"As research into autophagy has expanded, it has become clear it is not a response to starvation. It also contributes to a range of physiological functions, such as inhibiting cancer cells and aging, eliminating pathogens, and cleaning the insides of cells. We have also seen a small explosion in research that shows a new function with the knocking out genes that contribute to autophagy. However, there is still much we do not know about the mechanism of autophagy, and this calls for serious study."*

What Goes Behind?

We refer to autophagy as an evolutionary conserved cytoplasmic degradation process – the breakdown of cell organelles and the formation of newer, better cells. If we looked deeper and discuss the step-by-step process that results in anti-aging and other such health benefits, we'll learn that it is a 4-step process. In this process, a variety of materials are sequestered by a double-membrane structure known as an autophagosome. Once sequestered, they are then transferred to the lysosomes for the degradation. Because of the presence of several varieties of targets, autophagic activity is essential for cellular homeostasis.

This is clear through recent studies that showed a crucial impact of autophagy in regulating animal lifespan. Basic autophagic activity is elevated in many longevity patterns, and the activity is a must for lifespan extension. In most cases, lysosomal functions and autophagy, both involved genes, are induced by several transcription factors such as HLH-30/TFEB, PHA-4/FOXA, and MML-1/Mondo in long-lived animals.

Step 1: Sequestration

Autophagosome is formed around a cytoplasm and organelles.

Step 2: Transport to a lysosome

Autophagosome fuses with the lysosome

Step 3: Degradation

Lysosomes release enzymes that degrade material in Autophagosome

Step 4: Utilisation of Degradation Products

All cellular materials degrade to amino acids

Pharmacological treatments are now showing results of extended lifespans in both humans and animals because of the induction of autophagy or autophagic genes. It shows that autophagy could be a promising solution to modulate lifespan and aging.

Chapter 9
Autophagy and Blood Sugar

Lifestyle changes are immensely important where health issues are concerned, especially in the management of diseases such as type 2 diabetes. Scientists believe that intermittent fasting is the key to lowering the risk of such conditions. Let's get into the details of how autophagy addresses general health issues and impacts blood sugar levels.

With more and more advancement in medical sciences, it is surprising to find out the rising rates of several new diseases. Other than that, there are still some prevalent health issues dominating the world population in current times. One of them is diabetes.

Type 2 diabetes has reached epidemic proportions, affecting a sizeable majority of the world. It is a condition that affects the body's natural ability to produce insulin, which regulates blood sugar levels. Canada and the United States are both home to a large number of diabetic patients.

In the US, type 2 diabetes is one of the top reasons for death. For more information on how to illuminate diabetes with a diet and lifestyle proven step-by-step plan, go to eliminatediabetes.net

Eating habits contribute to a lifestyle which, in turn, decides one's health. A lifestyle can speed up your healing process from a particular disease and help you manage it. On the other hand, a poor lifestyle can lead to poor health and can also exacerbate existing medical conditions. For this reason, sedentary lifestyles are not advised to patients with tendencies of diabetes.

Doctors usually recommend patients with diabetes various diets. These diets restrict them from consuming certain foods and also ask them to make certain food items a part of their eating habit. The effects of such specific diets may vary from person to person. However, a diabetic person should avoid consuming processed foods, refined carbohydrates, and artificial sweeteners.

Diabetes mellitus or DM is an endocrine disorder; it is believed to become a leading cause of death across the globe in the coming years. Cellular injuries and disorders of energy metabolism are the two critical factors in the pathogenesis of diabetes. This leads to some severe diabetic complications and asks for autophagic intervention. It is known that autophagy plays a pivotal role in curing health diseases such as obesity, inflammation, cancer, diabetes, and such. Autophagy works on the principle of regulating the normal function of pancreatic β cells and targets the insulin-related tissues. Some of these tissues are adipose tissue, skeletal muscle, and liver. This chapter discusses the role of autophagy in managing diabetes. It also explains how autophagy and other therapeutic remedies help treat diabetes.

Intermittent Fasting and Diabetes

As per the Obesity Society, about 90 percent of people with type 2 diabetes are reported to be obese or overweight. Weight loss is one prominent treatment for type 2 diabetes that affects around 30.3 million people; it assists them with reduced insulin resistance and helps absorb blood glucose more effectively. Centers for Disease Control and Prevention (CDC) suggests that being overweight makes it difficult to regulate diabetes and is a risk factor for diabetes-related problems. \

The indicator of type 2 diabetes is insulin resistance, an illness in which the cells, muscles, and liver stop functioning effectively. This causes hyperglycemia (high blood sugar), and in extreme situations, requires medication, such as Glucophage and insulin, to lower blood sugar levels.

Regular calorie restriction through a restricted diet can eventually lead to weight loss and make it easier to control blood sugar. However, intermittent fasting is a step ahead by reducing serum insulin, which prompts the body to burn stored sugar, known as glycogen, along with fat. In recent times, there's a lot of research and debate on fasting. With every new research, more and more benefits are unearthed, revealing the many advantages of fasting for people – diabetic or not.

Autophagy tells us how our dietary patterns and lifestyle habits can impact our overall health. Autophagy is a way for cells to heal, strengthen, and refresh when they are not provided an external source of food – that is, the times that you stop eating. Jason Fung, a nutrition expert, discusses autophagy in these words: "By stimulating autophagy, we are clearing out all our old, junky proteins and cellular parts. At the same time, fasting also stimulates growth hormone, which tells our body to produce some new snazzy parts for the body. We are really giving our bodies the complete renovation." You might think about the importance of this procedure and ask yourself why our body needs cell renovation anyway.

Cell renovation occurs because our body cells age over time. They begin to break and divide and cease to grow, reducing their functionality and adding to the occupying space. These idle cells secrete inflammatory compounds that can damage the nearby cells. If not cleared up from the body, these dysfunctional cells can lead to several diseases. That's where autophagy comes into the picture, marking these cells and efficiently removing them from our bodies.

Autophagy is an increasingly important and prominent avenue of research as it can help fight such diseases as obesity, metabolic syndrome, and type 2 diabetes. However, if you're a diabetic patient, you must take a doctor's consultation before opting for autophagy. To get extensive information on diabetes and how to control it, visit eliminatediabetes.net

Autophagy And Its Impact On Type 2 Diabetes (T2D)

We discussed above that the process of autophagy helps regulate the pancreatic beta cells' function and insulin target tissues. According to the Centers for Disease Control and Prevention, over 30 million people in the US alone have a diabetic disorder. Of this number, over 90 to 95% have type 2 diabetes.

In diabetes, insulin, which helps control the amount of blood sugar within the body, becomes less effective. Also, cells fail to respond normally to insulin in a person with type 2 diabetes.

Lauri Wright, a Ph.D., serving as an assistant professor of public health at the University of South Florida explained in one of her interviews, "When we eat foods containing carbohydrates (bread, cereals, pasta, fruits, starchy vegetables, dairy), the body digests the carbohydrates into single sugars. The pancreas simultaneously receives a signal to release insulin. Insulin releases into the bloodstream and acts as a key to unlock the cells, allowing the single sugars to enter the cells and provide energy."

Because of reduced insulin functioning, which is what happens in type 2 diabetes, some single sugars accumulate in the cells. Thus, its ability to provide cells with energy drops. However, with the induction of autophagy, our body is forced to build its own insulin to meet the needs of the body. This helps restore the gap and strengthen its effect on blood sugar levels. Also, because of less calorie intake (most of the calories are consumed for daily activities), our body does not store food in any form. This helps the body remain undisturbed with any excess amount of blood sugar or glucose, leading to a reduced blood sugar level.

It is a well-known fact that high blood sugar can be hazardous for human health. It can damage the body's internal system, including metabolism, and can cause other health issues as well, such as vision loss, kidney problems, and heart diseases. Type 2 diabetes can be controlled and maintained through consuming a proper, healthy, and balanced diet with a vigorous exercise regime. Autophagy has proven to keep the body's natural function inflow by constantly regulating the blood sugar levels and maintaining overall health. In order to keep your fitness regime in check and up to date, check out myexerciseblog.com.

Chapter 10
Autophagy and Weight Loss

If you are looking for ways to lose weight faster and safer, you are right where you need to be. 'How to lose weight' seems to be a universal concern. Today, with celebrities advocating new trends of health, we all are becoming more and more aware of the benefits of staying fit.

In the current times, where the trend to stay fit has spread like wildfire, we are seeing newer solutions to the dilemma of weight loss in ways that are quicker as well as safer. Well, being fit and healthy is more than just being not-obese. It is about staying fit, both physically and mentally.

Fit people are healthier. They are not prone to most chronic diseases that are affecting the people of the United States. However, the question arises, 'How can we stay more fit?'

If you are looking for an answer to that, you are in the right place. This book will navigate your way through fitness loopholes and pitfalls that people run into, even though they try to stay healthy. Health and fitness have become a prominent concern in America because of the rising obesity rate and a reported increase in chronic diseases such as high blood pressures, high cholesterol levels, and diabetes. All these diseases, if not remedied, can lead to a slow death. This book discusses the improvements you can make to your everyday routine for better mental and physical health. Not many know that autophagy also helps improve cognitive brain performance.

To achieve a fit body, you need to get out of your set routine and walk the extra mile – literally as well as figuratively.

As discussed in the previous chapter, changes in lifestyle have the most significant impact on your health. You need to integrate exercise into your routine and also eat healthier, as these are two of the most common practices to induce autophagy. Apart from not eating for specific periods, you must spend adequate time outdoors doing physical activities, soaking up the sunlight while also burning some calories. Take part in activities such as hiking, sports, swimming, fishing, and bicycling.

Most times, we see people killing themselves on workout machines, sweating and overworking their muscles, running miles on end. But instead of losing weight, they end up losing hope at the end of the day. People give up their cravings for the sake of losing fat, keeping themselves in the state of fasting, but still end up nowhere.

This is because they do not channel their efforts in the right direction. There's no point in fasting for 18 hours and then hogging on loads of calories the moment your eating window opens.

The problem of losing weight is not only yours – there are thousands of others out there looking for the same answer. With the fluctuating trends, we also witnessed the trend of fat freezing. Then there was the 'keto diet' that took the world by a storm and led to the opening of several 'keto-friendly' gyms and restaurants. One such a modern method undiscovered by many is autophagy.

It is intermittent fasting that is used to enhance metabolism function, making it work longer hours and burning more and more fat content. Out of all the methods, autophagy has an advantage over the rest. Why? Because it produces faster, better, and safer results by working at a cellular level. So, what is it, and how to lose weight by getting onto it? By far, this book has established autophagy as a solution to most of your health-related problems. Based on that definition, let's look at the details of how autophagy plays a role in losing weight.

In simple words, intermittent fasting is the key. To achieve your desired body goals and harness the power that autophagy possesses, you need to follow the intermittent fasting regime religiously. This requires you to consume only a specific type of diet, and that too during a certain timeframe each day. You let the window open for only particular hours during the day and fast for the rest of the hours.

People, including celebrities, who are on autophagy consume a high protein diet during their open window (around 6 to 8 hours) and let their bodies do the work for the next 16 to 18 hours. That's when your metabolism breaks down food for energy. This not only helps you lose weight but also improves hair and skin quality as claimed by many already practicing it.

Autophagy Supports Healthy Weight

Autophagy, as we all know by now, supports healthy weight regulation. Below are some important benefits of autophagy that support healthy weight loss:

The process of autophagy catalyzes the fat burning process but also spares the protein any damage – meaning there is no loss of muscle mass. On extended fasts, you are prone to lose protein mass. However, in autophagy, which does not require fasting for that long, only fat-burning takes place. And you get to enjoy all the benefits of leaner, fitter self through protein preservation!

Autophagy also treats any unnecessary inflammation. Chronic inflammation is one of the rising diseases due to several reasons, such as the ubiquity of a sedentary lifestyle. Chronic inflammation is linked to increased insulin, which leads to more weight storage. Reduced inflammation means lesser insulin levels and less fat storage.

Autophagy removes toxins from your cells. As long as these toxins are secreted, there will be no need for fat cells to store them. Besides that, autophagy also supports metabolic efficiency. Metabolic efficiency refers to the process of cell repairing that makes and packages protein and processes energy. This is specifically helpful when cells need to switch to the fat-burning process for energy.

Intermittent Fasting and Its Stages!

Intermittent fasting has several cycles of inter-bodily processes that occur at different periods of fasting. For instance, by the time you have reached 12 hours of fasting, you enter a metabolic state known as ketosis. During ketosis, your body breaks down stored fat packets and burns them to produce the energy required by the body.

The liver uses some of this fat in the production of ketone bodies. When glucose supply is not readily available to the body, ketones serve as an alternative source for the brain cells and other necessary tissues. While in the resting state, your brain consumes up to 60% of your body's glucose level. Ketone bodies generated by the liver (through fat burning) partially substitute for glucose by acting as a replacement fuel for the brain and other organs during the fast. The ketone usage by the brain reinforces the fact that autophagy and intermittent fasting promote a better mental state. To familiarize yourself with more keto-related information, check out, myketoblog.net. By the time your fast duration reaches 18 hours, you enter the fat-burning mode as now your body's ketone generation levels have grown significantly. As the ketone level in the body rises, they act like hormones in the body – as signaling molecules. For instance, they indicate the body to increase stress-busting pathways that help to reduce inflammation and repair damaged DNA as well.

Check this link for more information: myketoblog.net

By the time the fast reaches hits 24 hours of duration, your body cells recycle old components and break down misfolded proteins linked to some severe diseases like Alzheimer's. This is where autophagy kickstarts. It is an essential procedure for cell rejuvenation. However, when the body experiences difficulty in achieving autophagy, it can lead to harms such as neurodegenerative diseases.

The Mammalian Target of Rapamycin (mTOR) activates Autophagy. This is initiated through fasting, which activates the AMPK signaling pathway and inhibits mTOR activity. By the time your fast reaches a stage of 48 hours with no intake of energy (in the form of calories, carbs, or proteins, etc.) from any external source, your growth hormone levels shoot up as high as five times since the time you started fasting. This could partially be because ketone bodies produced during fasting promote growth hormones secretion – for instance, in the brain. Ghrelin, commonly known as the hunger hormone, also boosts the release of growth hormones.

Growth hormones help preserve the protein mass by preserving lean muscle and work to reduce fat tissue accumulation, especially as we grow older. They also promote wound healing and cardiovascular diseases.

Autophagy is a biological process that you can easily manipulate for weight loss if you understand the triggers and are willing to make serious lifestyle changes and adopt eating habits that support the process. By modifying your diet, you can further fix the autophagy process, making it easier to shed unwanted weight and make other metabolic processes more efficient.

Chapter 11
Autophagy and
Inflammation

With various direct and indirect benefits that autophagy entails, it also offers great help in reducing inflammation. As per research from the Severance Biomedical Science Institute and the Department of Internal Medicine, autophagy is a self-degradation process. In the process of development and response to nutrient stress, autophagy plays a crucial role in balancing the sources of energy. Besides that, autophagy works on removing aggregated or misfolded proteins.

The process helps in clearing damaged organelles such as endoplasmic reticulum, mitochondria, and peroxisomes. Not just that, but it also helps to eliminate intercellular pathogens. Therefore, autophagy is linked to a survival mechanism, even though its deregulation connects with non–apoptotic cell death. In simple words, it means that during the process of autophagy, the cells become stronger as well as clean and efficient.

However, when it deregulates, it may trigger unusual forms of cell destruction. But it is not only the cells that benefit from autophagy. There are other subprocesses, which autophagy influences. On a micro-organic level, autophagy reduces inflammation in the body — inflammation results from cellular breakdown. We can understand the effect of inflammation on the body in such a way that chronic inflammation to a human body is what water is to electronic devices. Unlike mild and acute inflammation, chronic inflammation can have long-term effects on the whole body, affecting not only the external body but also long-term wellbeing. It interferes with internal body systems and blocks many regulatory health processes.

We also refer to chronic inflammation as low-grade, persistent inflammation. This is because of its unique nature of producing a gradual and steady inflammation throughout the body. According to a study published in Johns Hopkins Health Review, this systematic inflammation can cause several consequential diseases. Chronic inflammation can be a barrier, restricting many of the body's natural processes from occurring at its usual smooth pace. It may also result in severe chronic damage. Autophagy keeps not only cells in good shape but also helps prevent inflammation from happening in the first place. Autophagy has much more to offer than just weight loss. As a constituent element of longevity and extended health, autophagy serves as a constant shield against inflammation. According to the study above, strong autophagy is the "key in preventing diseases such as cancer, neurodegeneration, cardiomyopathy, diabetes, liver disease, autoimmune diseases, and infections."

However, the silver lining to this cloud is the possibility of practical techniques and their implementation through therapies, techniques, and daily habits. Through these, individuals can put their bodies on the right track by boosting their ability to execute autophagy.

The Science Behind Reduced Inflammation and Autophagic Impact

In its purest form, autophagy is an essential process of homeostasis – a process through which it degrades cytoplasmic components in a double membrane-bound autophagosome. This is in response to starvation, which is the basis for autophagy. Paradoxically, where autophagy acts as a shield for many of the cells' functions, it is also responsible for the death of cells. However, this does not have any negative impact on the overall human body; the process is essential and pans out positively.

Autophagy plays a key role in bridging the two platforms – innate and adaptive immune systems. Doctors associate dysfunctional autophagy with inflammation, neurodegeneration, cancer, and infection.

As we discussed, the autophagic homeostatic mechanism revolves around disposing of damaged subcellular particles and organelles, denatured proteins, and invaded pathogens. This is done through a lysosomal degradation pathway. Its role, as brought to light by scientists, is linking innate and adaptive immunity. This is the reason behind the influence of pathogenesis in inflammatory diseases.

Through its influential intervention on development, autophagy plays a critical role in inflammation. This process includes the transcription disruption, processing, and secretion of several cytokines.

With autophagy reaching new heights of research and experimentation, its dependent subjects were recently studied in the pathogenesis of several inflammatory diseases. This included infectious diseases, cystic fibrosis, chronic obstructive pulmonary diseases, Crohn's diseases, and others. These studies resulted in suggestive modulation of autophagy, which might lead to therapeutic interventions for inflammation-related diseases.

Autophagy and its consequences were first discovered as the metabolic and cytoplasmic quality control processes. However, the role of autophagy in the light of research and study has evolved over the last couple of years. With modern studies, we find the role of autophagy growing over the last decade. These connections are a hint that links to further passages of the network and association that lie between metabolism, inflammation, quality control, and immunity processes. Immunity processes are essential to many human diseases such as neurodegenerative diseases, diabetes, chronic inflammation, cancer, aging, and infections.

Key Points

- Autophagy is a fundamental eukaryotic pathway influential on innate and adaptive immunity pathways. Autophagic responses are integrated with recognition receptor and cytokine signaling.

- Sequestosome 1–like receptors (autophagic receptors) target intercellular microorganisms for autophagic purposes through ubiquitin and galectin tags. They represent a new pattern recognition receptor niche.

- Intercellular pathogens evolve and possess much-elaborated strategies. They shield and neutralize autophagy for its own survival.

- Autophagy inhibits inflammasome activation, which modulates type–1 interferon responses.

- Autophagy is a potent anti-inflammatory process.

- Autophagy plays a part in the secretion of antimicrobial and inflammatory mediators.

- Autophagy affects conventional phagosome maturation by enhancing it. It affects T cell homeostasis and T helper cell polarization.

- There is a genetic and physiological link between autophagy and inflammatory diseases in humans.[6]

What is acute inflammation? Acute inflammation refers to the part of the host's innate recoil response to protect from infections and tissue injury. If breached, endothelial cell injury or microbial infection causes changes to the vascular permeability and the distribution of chemoattractants.

Unusually high or diverging inflammatory responses are associated with a wide range of chronic, acute, and systematic inflammatory disorders. This may include asthma, cardiovascular diseases, rheumatoid arthritis, inflammatory bowel diseases, and cystic fibrosis.

As per recent studies, we have discovered that macroautophagy plays an influential role in the host during bacterial clearance. Autophagy impacts inflammatory processes, henceforth affecting the outcome of disease progression.[7]

Inducing autophagy becomes active during starvation. A

––––––––––––––––––––––––

[6] https://www.nature.com/articles/nri3532
[7] https://www.hindawi.com/journals/ijcb/2011/732798/

study suggested that autophagy usually kicks into high gear during times of stress to protect the body (such as in times of famine). These high-stress responses may include protein aggregates, DNA damage, reactive oxygen species, and intercellular pathogens, etc. When we activate autophagy, it slows down the aging process in the most natural way possible. It reduces inflammation in the body and boosts our overall natural ability to function properly. It helps our body develop a defensive shield against diseases and promote longevity. Once established, we can increase our autophagy response naturally with time.

Fasting is known to be the number one booster of activating autophagy in the human body. For instance, if you skip meals for 18 hours, your body switches to fat-burning mode. It generates significant ketones, pushing you into ketosis. Ketones act as signaling molecules by the time their number level increases within the body. Similar to hormones, they command your body to ramp up stress-busting pathways, which repairs damaged DNA and reduces inflammation. We should limit our protein intake to 15-30 grams per day twice or thrice a week, depending on the circumstances.

This will give our body a full day to recycle the proteins. Recycling proteins helps reduce inflammation and cleanse it, causing no muscle loss.

Although autophagy is still a topic under research, there is increasing evidence that suggests it plays a critical role in the development of inflammation pathogenesis and immunity response.

Chapter 12
Autophagy and
Detoxification

The concept of detoxification is not new for medical science. From Ayurvedic and Chinese medicine to modern-day western medicine, detoxification is practiced by many cultures and religions for centuries. In short, detoxification is about resting, cleansing, nourishing, and replenishing the body from the inside out. Through following the process of removing toxins from your body and refueling it with healthy nutrients, detoxification helps as a shield against many diseases. Besides that, it renews your ability to maintain optimum health with a range of practices involved.

How Does Detoxification Work?

In its simplest forms, as the term suggests, detoxification means to detoxify or to clean harmful toxins. This is done by removing impurities from the blood in the liver, where the most toxin accumulation takes place. Besides that, the body also works towards discarding any impurities or remnants of toxins from intestines, lymphatic system, kidneys, skin, lungs, etc. However, in circumstances of these systems being compromised, impurities are partially retained, which leads to an adverse situation.

A detoxification program can help the body's natural cleansing process in several ways. Some of which are:

- Fasting – resting your organs through fasting is the most efficient and least harmful way.
- Stimulating the liver into driving toxins out.
- Promoting the elimination of toxins through skin, intestines, and kidneys.
- Improving blood regulation.
- Nourishing body with healthy nutrients.

"Detoxification works because it addresses the needs of individual cells, the smallest units of human life," says Peter Bennett, N.D., co-author of *7-Day Detox Miracle* with Stephen Barrie, N.D., and Sara Faye

The world has seen many misleading health trends and malpractice of selling dust in the name of health and nutrition. Detox or detoxification was not spared either. The new buzzword "Detox" took both the worlds of glam and the health industry by storm. However, the word was probably the most overused and misunderstood. The greatest offenders of this statement would be the purveyors of detox products (smoothies and other fancy food in the name of health). The simplest way to know this is to calculate the calories most of these 'healthy' detox smoothies contain. It will probably amount to a can of fizzy drink. Furthermore, the amount and type of sugar used in these concoctions do the opposite of detoxification.

Fructose metabolism is the opposite of glucose. Glucose can quickly be processed and broken down into enzymes, while fructose is very difficult to metabolize and processes only in the liver. The diet trends advocated by these nutritionists in the modern day are rich in fructose levels. These normalized diets create hindrances for your body's primary detoxifying function.

However, this chapter will reveal some facts that might go against what we usually perceive as 'the only method' to detoxify the body of harmful toxins. The reality is opposite to these mainstream beliefs. To detoxify your body, instead of stuffing it with more and more food with added substances that aid to intoxication, stop eating. Yes, you heard it right.

The best way to detoxify is to stop providing your body with any excess food supply.

Role of Autophagy in Detoxification

The process of detoxification is immensely vital for us, from clearing out the harmful bacteria to increase lifespan. One of the most efficient and least damaging ways to get rid of the harmful toxins and chemicals in your body is through autophagy.

Through consuming foreign invaders (or encouraging the body's immune system to get rid of it), autophagy helps our cells get rid of all the harmful substances that have accumulated in our systems. These harmful cells are a potential threat to human health as they can cause inflammation and damage to the cell structure.

One example of the part played by autophagy in detoxification is the removal of ammonia. As per studies, autophagy removes ammonia from the liver causing no threats, while also preventing it from accumulating inside the organ.

Gastronomy and Detoxification

Fructose poses the same threat to the liver as alcohol and other toxins do. The rise of an increase in fatty liver diseases over the past few years can be justified through the statistics that suggest fructose consumption has gone 400 times higher in the last couple of decades. On average, 1 out of every three adults in the US suffers from non-alcoholic fatty liver disease.

So dump that cup of 'detox smoothie' you are probably planning on drinking, it's time to go clean!

This does not mean that detoxification cannot be achieved through diet changes; it can. In this chapter, however, we are discussing a better and much more effective way of detoxification of harmful toxins, and that is through autophagy.

Factors That Affect Autophagy and Detoxification

Primary factors that halt the process of autophagy are the consumption of carbohydrates and subsequent hormone insulin production.

This nullifies all the claims of health and fitness websites that market fresh press juices, quinoa bowls, green salads, and such stuff in the name of boosting the detoxification process when all it does is just turn off your cellular detoxification process at the deepest level.

The same goes for natural and artificial sweeteners. Plus, there's also a need to avoid excess protein consumption. The presence of amino acid *leucine* can disrupt or may completely kick autophagy off. However, this does not imply that you should restrict protein to the same extent as you would the carbs and sugars.

The Bottom Line

A gentle detox bath is one of the great ways you can channel your body to detoxify and get rid of some toxins. However, if you are serious about setting your body on detoxing mode, autophagy is your key to getting there. This natural process is an amazing way not just to get rid of the harmful body toxins but also to encourage cellular homeostasis. The human body, although complicated, is adaptive and smart. Autophagy is a genius way the body works in adapting to dealing with stressors and improving cellular health. An added benefit of autophagy, as compared to other options, is that it is readily available and anyone can adopt it. There's no involvement of expensive equipment or any supplements. All you need to do is restrict your food supply for specific time durations, creating small stressors that ultimately boost health.

As we have talked about before, there is nothing wrong with drinking your weight in liquid kale. Autophagy is our advanced answer and an evolved strategy to detoxify. Fasting is one of the most effective ways of inducing autophagy, which serves as a purpose of central therapy for detoxification. It is a healing method centered on the principles that illnesses and many prolonged diseases occur because of the accumulation of toxic substances in the body.

Fasting primarily follows a fundamental law that is straightforward. By temporarily halting food intake, it allows our bodies a break from the continuous process of breaking down food particles into enzymes and producing chemical energy. That extra time for the body gives it a boost and the chance to replenish, heal, and restore itself. This is the downtime required for the body to detoxify itself. Fasting also burns previously-stored calories (which by then become fat tissues), which work as a catalyst to remove the stored toxic substances in our body. The detoxification process, followed by our digestive system accompanied by our metabolism, goes something like this. Our digestive tract is an organ most exposed to environmental threats, including harmful bacteria, contagious viruses, parasites, and toxins. And so, it requires the support of the immune system the most.

After being broken down into small particles in the intestines, food travels through our blood to the liver, which is the largest organ of the human body's natural detoxification system. The liver furthers the process by breaking it down and filtering out the toxic by-products released during digestion. It includes both toxins, the natural ones, and the chemical ones, present in the chemically processed foods that we consume. During fasting, the liver and immune system are essentially liberated to detoxify and heal other parts of the body.

Autophagy is a cellular recycling process that removes previously damaged or broken-down cells. This frees up some space for new cells to form in your body, resulting in reduced inflammation. It also counters severe health issues such as diabetes, insulin resistance, Alzheimer's, cardiovascular diseases, and even aging. The real endeavor here is to channel this natural process of detoxification and cleaning within your body for maximal health benefits without overdoing it and experiencing unnecessary stress.

Chapter 13
Autophagy and
Diseases/Ailments

Most of us don't know it, but our cells could use some cleaning up. This idea sets the base for cellular progression and its respective movement in infectious diseases. We refer to the process as Autophagy. The mechanism of autophagy follows the recycling of essential nutrients in order to eliminate harmful pathogens from the body.

Almost a century ago, Christian de Duve coined the term "Autophagy." The term is derived from Greek, and its literal meaning is 'self-eating.' It implies a cell degradation process where cells devour their cytoplasmic materials within lysosomes.

As we keep progressing with time, autophagy has become the subject of scientific research. Enjoying the limelight, scientists made more and more new developments in the subject. By now, we have defined three major types of autophagy: micro-autophagy (cytoplasmic engulfing by lysosomes through inward invagination of the lysosomal membrane); macroautophagy (characterized by the formation of distinctive double-membrane organelle known as autophagosome); and chaperone-mediated autophagy.[8] Autophagy, the known cellular cleaning process, is induced or triggered through certain metabolic stresses. These stresses may include hypoxia, nutrient deprivation, and growth factor depletion. With no adequate circulation, each cell may break down into further sub-cellular particles and recycle them to create new protein for fuel for the body. This reinforces the explanation of why mTOR and autophagy go hand in hand in every organism, from yeast to human beings.

Several studies have been carried out by now that confirm the importance of autophagy for survival and longevity. It indirectly emphasizes that autophagy helps fight several diseases that build up over time, resulting in early death. Autophagy is an age reversal mechanism. The deletion of autophagy-related genes in animals, plants, and other test objects has been found to risk life competency through several kinds of research. This highlights the importance of autophagy for survival and disease prevention on earth.

---

[8] https://www.nature.com/articles/cr2013161

ATGs or autophagic genes regulate mainly through Insulin and Amino Acids when we consume carbohydrates, our insulin level increases. Whereas when we consume proteins, both the insulin and mTOR levels rise. When nutrient sensors sense these shifting patterns, they signal the body for a reaction, which is to grow. Thus, nutrient sensors turn off autophagy or block the autophagic process from occurring. This results in the activation of an anabolic process instead of a catabolic process (breaking down of food and particles). Autophagy helps prevent diseases by acting as a cellular housekeeper.[9]

Autophagy and Pathogen Prevention!

Autophagy switches to maintenance mode in the body when things are running smoothly. This means autophagy occurs at a low cellular level in worn-out recycling cells under no or minimum metabolic stress. But when the body undergoes metabolic stress such as nutrient deficiency or lack of energy or microbe invasion, the strengthened autophagic response gets activated. We know this as a stress

---

[9] https://www.marksdailyapple.com/7-ways-to-induce-autophagy/

response. Let's discuss some severe diseases experienced by many people and understand the role autophagy plays in preventing them.

Neurodegeneration

Many neurodegenerative diseases result from disordered or damaged proteins accumulated in and around the neurons. This is linked with examples of psychiatric disorders as the accumulated damaged proteins induce gradual death of brain cells, resulting in subsequent loss of mental faculties. Since autophagy is a cellular cleaning process, it helps to clean these worn-out proteins and replace them with fresh ones.

Liver Diseases

The quality control of protein functions is essential in the pathogenesis of the most prevalent genetic causes of human liver diseases linked with chronic inflammation and carcinogenesis. Similar to neurodegenerative diseases induced by aggregate-prone proteins, pharmacological activation of autophagy may be useful in this case.

Psychiatric Disorders

A typical autophagic process provides help against the progression of several psychiatric disorders. The disruption of the autophagic process disruption or absence of ATGs is linked with an increased risk of some known psychiatric conditions such as depression (triggering negative thoughts and anxiety) and schizophrenia.

Infectious Diseases

There are three ways in which autophagy helps to fight infectious diseases, which are:

- Toxin removal which is created by infections
- Xenophagy-removal of microbes from inside cells
- Immune response modulation to infections

Autophagy helps in removing infectious microbes, protozoans, viruses, and HIV, etc.

Inflammation

Chronic inflammation can be a barrier, restricting many of the body's natural processes from occurring at its usual smooth pace. It may also result in severe chronic damage.

Autophagy keeps not only cells in good shape but also helps prevent inflammation from happening in the first place.

Autophagy helps to reduce inflammation, which results in an immune response. Besides that, autophagy also helps to remove pro-immune response molecules produced by the cells.

Increased Muscle Performance

When we exercise, our body undergoes severe muscular stress. This stress results in small ruptures or punctures in muscle fibers. However, this boosts the autophagic process, which then helps to:

- Balance energy within cells and maintaining it
- Ensure the removal of damaged or degraded cellular components before they cause problems.
- Recycle existing energy molecules more efficiently by keeping energy for over a longer time

Cancer

Autophagy, to some extent, prevents and suppresses spreading cancer cellular activity. It is highly effective in inhibiting the early growth of cancer. It suppresses chronic inflammation, genome instability, and DNA damage responses. As per research, mice that were genetically tested with the absence of autophagic activators (or genes) were reported to have a high threat to cancer.

However, autophagy's protective cellular mechanism may also be hijacked by some progressed tumors. Tumors isolate the cells as it progresses in the body, restraining it from reaching the blood supply needed to undergo energy and nutrient stress. However, to some extent, activation of autophagy can provide a shield against these cancerous cells. Autophagy seems to be very beneficial in playing its part before the cancer cells have fully developed in the body.

Skin Diseases

Since autophagy is a process of pathogen component degradation, it helps find most of the conjugated skin and cellular diseases. Autophagy promotes both the survival and death of infected or damaged cells. This is done through the delivery of TLRs (Toll-Like Receptors) ligands to endosomes to activate innate immunity.

Psoriasis

Psoriasis is an immune-mediated inflammatory disease that falls under the category of chronic skin diseases. This plague has affected almost over 3 percent of the world's total population, which is a high number of affected people. This cellular disorder is influenced by both environmental and genetic factors. Psoriasis is characterized by epidermal proliferation and inflammation.

Several plaguing pathogens, such as fungi, viruses, and bacteria, are linked to psoriasis. The strongest association occurs with tonsillar *Streptococcus pyogenes* infection, which connects to the development of guttate psoriasis and can persist as chronic plaque psoriasis. Autophagy helps to eliminate such bacteria. Thus, it is very important to induce autophagy in the case of psoriasis. Otherwise, it can lead to altered immune responses to bacteria.

Melanoma

In metastatic melanoma, the autophagy capacity is re-established, which provides for the high metabolic demands for cancer cells. It supports survival in the face of the stressful tumor microenvironment. The knockdown of key autophagic genes, such as Beclin1 and ATG7, triggers the spontaneous elimination of melanoma cells. Besides that, it reduces the clonogenic expansion of metastatic melanoma cells.[10]

Diabetes

Autophagy plays a pivotal role in curing health diseases such as obesity, inflammation, cancer, diabetes, and such. It works on the principle of regulating the normal function of pancreatic β cells and targets insulin-related tissues. Some of these tissues are adipose tissue, skeletal muscle, and liver.

However, this is not it. Several other studies analyze the role of autophagy in healing and prevention from chronic diseases. For now, researchers are more focused on understanding the role of autophagy in death-promoting and survival-support; how the natural receptors interact with autophagic compounds with the activation of autophagy to either induce or inhibit its effect. More detailed studies are being carried out on the underlying pharmacological impact and evaluation of autophagy. Modern medical facilities

---

[10] https://www.karger.com/Article/FullText/500470

promote autophagy-inducing natural products and highlight some fundamental benefits along with their usage under guided prescription, such as duration, dose, consequences, caution, prevention, and conventional therapies.

Expanding our horizons of medical research and studies, autophagy-related genes play a pivotal role in addressing some modern threats faced by humanity, such as the Zika Virus. Zika stems from the same family as of West Nile and Dengue, and Bencilin1 (s discussed above) seems to play a mutual restorative role in both the scenarios – in the stabilization of cell organelles and coordinated healthy neural development.

As viruses keep on emerging and the threat of antibiotic-resistant bacteria grows, researchers are viewing autophagy as an enhancement or a potent tool to defend against such lethal diseases in the future.[11]

---

[11] https://www.nature.com/articles/nm0416-334

Chapter 14
Ways to Induce Autophagy

Autophagy is our body's way of recycling and rejuvenating cells. It clears out damaged cells and replaces them with new, fresh, and healthier ones.

Our internal biological systems have a self-maintenance mechanism. Doctors may perform a biological examination, but even that's external. This reinforces the phenomena that for life to maintain itself. It needs to perform automatic self-care or self-maintenance on its cells, organs, and tissues. One of the most important types of such processes is known as Autophagy.

Autophagy provides long-term benefits to the human body, such as prevention from chronic diseases and anti-aging (or slow aging). However, it has some instant effects as well, such as weight loss. You should see the benefits of autophagy within two weeks of starting the process.

The average person in today's society consumes an industrial meal and rarely goes long enough without consuming something that triggers autophagy. They are also not spending enough energy to create an energy deficit from the other end — the output. If our ancestors were to exist in this current scenario, many of them would go gaga overexploiting the advantage of the modern food environment. But that doesn't make it desirable or right for you. It just means that figuring out how to trigger autophagy becomes that much more vital for modern humans.

Autophagy usually kicks into high gear during times of stress, to protect the body (such as in times of famine). When we activate autophagy, it slows down the aging process in the most natural way possible. It reduces inflammation in the body and boosts our overall natural ability to function correctly. It helps our body develop a defensive shield against diseases and promote longevity. Once established, we can increase our autophagy response naturally with time.

There are several ways to induce autophagy within the body without seeking the help of any fancy and expensive detox smoothies or juice cleansers. The autophagic process is critical to keep your body running in its optimum health, with reduced levels of inflammation, cell cleansing, and prevention from many diseases. Let's discuss some ways and changes in lifestyle patterns that cannot just help induce autophagy, but also to maintain it for more extended periods as a habit or practice. Just keep in mind that you need to trick your body into thinking it's a little under pressure since autophagy itself is a stress response activity.

Fasting

There is no better way to induce a significant energy deficit paradigm other than fasting. Fasting has proven to be one of the quickest and most reliable sources of shifting dietary patterns without causing the body any harm.

There is no 'defined' or preset definition of 'optimal' fasting and the guidelines to follow for autophagic induction. Fasting is basically restraining your body from consuming any external food source.

Fasting (or intermittent fasting) brings about pronounced health benefits such as longevity, weight loss, and decreased risk for heart diseases and diabetes. Scientists have conducted studies to discover the optimum health benefits of fasting. They observed lab monkeys and mice that fast in lab experiments to have a healthy lifespan and live longer than the ones regularly fed. Besides that, fasting is not just restricting food or water intake.

There are several types of fasting – each distinctive to serve their own purpose (please refer to previous chapters for reference). While longer fasting periods allow deeper levels of autophagic induction, shorter fasts are also effective. Intermittent fasting involves cycling between periods of fasting and eating, ranging from a few hours to a few days at a time.

By skipping breakfast, and consuming most of your daily meals within the 8-hour window, you can boost up your body's internal autophagy process. Just as protein-specific fasting, intermittent fasting allows your body to 'catch up' on all those prevailing toxins lingering around your body by cleaning them up in real-time. With 16 to 28 hour fasting, we can remove harmful toxins out of our body.

However, there are some complications involved, for women specifically, if not done right. Fasting may create a hormonal imbalance. To prevent that from happening, take precautionary measures by consuming a fat-only breakfast, i.e., bulletproof coffee. By keeping your bodies deprived of carbs and proteins, you remain in a fasting state, letting your fat cells do all the work.

Autophagy and Ketosis

Ketosis, as discussed previously, is a metabolic process in which body cells use up the stored fat and glucose as the first form of energy. Ketosis demands restricting your intake of carbohydrates and sugars.

Glucose is derived from dietary carbohydrates such as sugar and starch-containing food such as bread or pasta. These complex sugars are broken down in the body into simple sugars. Glucose is an essential component that can be stored into the liver or muscles in an inactive form known as glycogen. The body adapts to alternative strategies to meet the need for energy in the body. When the need arises, glycogen releases in an active form of glucose and ketones are formed as a by-product.

In ketosis, we switch the fuel channel for the body by starving it of carbs. We push our bodies to consume fats to burn as a primary source of producing energy. This is the magic that goes behind a ketogenic diet. The body achieves ketosis after a certain amount of time into intermittent fasting. You take lesser time to start the autophagy process when you are on a keto or fat-adapted diet. You are already halfway there. Within 24 hours of fasting, your body shifts from ketosis to autophagy, where your cells increasingly recycle old compounds and particles. This process breaks down the misfolded proteins that link to severe diseases such as Alzheimer's. Ketogenic diet increases the fat intake while reducing carbohydrate consumption, resulting in the shift of energy channel from glucose to ketones. This dietary and metabolic shift that occurs because of Fasting leads to autophagy. It is an excellent way of inducing autophagy for people who struggle with calorie restriction or fasting. Don't forget to check out myketoblog.net for some great insight on the keto diet.

Here's more on Keto: myketoblog.net

Exercise and Train Harder

As discussed previously, you can induce autophagy in two ways, with or without fasting. However, exercise is a must, whether you fast or not. When fasting, you need not go overboard with exercising. However, in a non-fasting state, you may have to concentrate more on burning some calories with extensive exercising. Exercise increases autophagy levels by decreasing insulin levels and, thus, growing glucagon to induce autophagy. Induce autophagy through HIIT (High-Intensity Interval Training): HIIT is another beneficial way of inducing autophagy. Let's recall some previous principles and base our explanation on that. We discussed that autophagy is a bodily response to stress. When we opt for high-intensity training or integrate some intensive exercise in our daily life routine, we put our bodies under the good stress spot. This means that the body undergoes just enough stress to trigger biochemical change within. You get the required boost to get your muscles to grow stronger without being harmed. For starters, aim for at least or approximately 20 to 30 minutes of HIIT to give an optimal boost to your longevity. With myexerciseblog.com, maintain a healthy lifestyle, and also a healthy body.

Get Restorative Sleep

Take some rest and have a good night's sleep; your body knows how to clear cells even when you are asleep. As per the tests conducted by Whittle, humans possess either one of the four sleeping personalities. These personalities inform the way we function throughout the day and night. Yes, you can reap the benefits of autophagy while you are asleep.

Knowing which sleep personality you have can help you induce autophagy through your circadian rhythms or sleep-wake cycles.

Autophagy and Diet

Eating healthy does not have to be complicated. If you feel overwhelmed by all the conflicting and confusing diet advice and nutrition guides out there, then you are not alone. The shift in calorie sources also results in the change of metabolic pathways. Through fasting and ketosis, one can put fat on the track of producing energy instead of carbohydrate-driven glucose.

Low glucose levels link to lower insulin and high glucagon levels, which you can achieve through a shift in dietary pattern. Previously, we discussed several ways to get into autophagy without forcing yourself to fast. Understandably, some people struggle very hard with fasting; thus, instead of doing that, you can achieve autophagy by being selective about what you eat. When you consume a diet low on sugar levels through ketosis or intermittent fasting, your body undergoes positive stress that wakes up the survival repairing mode.

When we speak of ketogenic or any other diets that help to induce autophagy, we are specifically targeting diets high in fat content and low in carbs. The shift of burning ketones from burning glucose in such a diet mimics a naturally occurring process of fasting – and thus, increases autophagy in its own time. Besides that, there are some additional steps or dietary changes that you can adopt to induce and catalyze autophagic processes, such as:

- Drink coffee: Coffee speeds up the autophagy process in the liver, heart, and muscle tissue. This effect remains for a longer duration when coffee (caffeinated or decaffeinated both) is given Ad libitum food.
- Eat turmeric: Curcumin, found in turmeric, is specifically very effective in inducing autophagy in mitochondria.
- Consume extra virgin olive oil
- Go on a protein fast: Limit your protein intake to twice or thrice a week and keep it at 20 or 25 grams only. This will give your body the full space to

recover and recycle damaged proteins and will help reduce inflammation through cell cleansing.

Chapter 15
The Workbook

Since autophagy is a form of self–cannibalism, the correct implementation and the right set of tools are the two main determinants of how effective any diet could be.

You may be working hard, restricting yourself from consuming extra carbs and fats, and running miles. At the day end, however, you reach nowhere. Why is that? Why is it that none of your efforts make a significant impact, as they should? Why is it that your regular diet is lying to you?

Well, the problem lies in the roots! We just fail to recognize it. We are working hard rather than smart. All that we need to do is channel our efforts in the right direction to enjoy the health goals we want.

Autophagy is one such modern concept that is gaining traction as a solution to significant health and weight issues. By now, we are acquainted with the basic idea and the mechanisms that lie behind autophagy. The question that arises now is: how to practice it? Well, for starters, your body needs to go under some hardship since autophagy is a stress-generated response. The process of autophagy follows the cliché statement: "Short term discomfort can bring long-term benefits." With working on autophagy, many people take the shortcut by not going through the hardships and the long-term diet plan changes. This can be a daunting step to take with no prior guidance. However, to address such clients, drug companies are already working on creating pharmaceutical solutions to stimulate autophagy.

You might have come across some 'health and fitness' bloggers who claim to stimulate the process of autophagy through certain supplements. Trust me; it's a hoax! The only proven way to trigger autophagy is through fasting. It is by restricting the body from consuming additional food rather than consuming more 'supplements' to induce it.

Several methods to do so have been discussed extensively in the previous chapters. In this chapter, we will talk about some practices to keep you on a healthy track while embracing autophagy. Mainly, autophagy occurs when you continue to live a healthy lifestyle. If you time your eating and restrict yourself from ingesting processed food high in calories, you can easily achieve autophagy. Develop an exercise regime and practice it daily. Occasionally, go hard on your physical training routine by integrating High-Intensity Interval Training (HIIT). Have a good night's sleep – yes, you can burn calories even when you are asleep! Recover well. Do not consume extra carbohydrates that your body does not require. Incorporate healthy greens and more liquids in your diets, such as green tea and black coffee (even decaf). Do not overeat at any hour, thinking you will burn it later off – or if you do, make sure you burn it before you go to bed.

Even if you are not practicing autophagy as a daily habit, make sure you take out some time and have some big autophagy sessions now and then. While designing your 'training session,' incorporate sprints and strength training. Lots of intense bursts are viable in triggering autophagy. To give a boost to autophagy, try fasting. Fasting is undoubtedly the best way to induce autophagy. Stay busy throughout your fast, so you do not indulge your food cravings and burn your calories. Even if you are not doing hard strength training, just going off the extra mile with your daily tasks can bring about the results you are seeking! Go out on a walk, and by this, I don't mean to roam around aimlessly. Brisk walk for at least 40 to 60 minutes on an empty stomach to boost your calorie-burning process. Walking while fasting will ramp up the fat burning process and will get you into ketosis quickly.

How to Practice Fasting?

In recent years, intermittent fasting has been very trendy. It is also enjoying the spotlight in the fitness field. Its acclaimed benefits include positive weight loss, improved metabolism, and extended lifespan. Due to its rising popularity, the term is associated with several types of methods for practicing it.

I will not contradict any of the proposed theories as many of them work in their own ways and are actually very useful. But it is primarily up to the person to opt for the most suitable method that works the best for them. Always choose the diet you think you can stick to for a long time.

A ketogenic diet is one of the most renowned methods of inducing autophagy, as it restricts you from consuming carbs. Foods low in carbs and high in fat are much more effective in inducing autophagy. You can also practice protein fasting by going on a complete 24-hour fast twice or thrice a week.

To get started with intermittent fasting, one of the primary steps anyone can take easily, without affecting their daily routine, is to skip breakfast. Skip your breakfast and consume all of your calories within an 8-hour window. The point to remember here is to not go over the limit and eat whatever you like. You need to count your daily caloric intake and ensure you limit it.

The key takeaway is to restrict carbohydrates occasionally, fast twice a week at least, and follow your regular exercise regime. All these habits bring about a multitude of benefits in addition to their impact on autophagy. This way, you will get a stronger, leaner, and younger body.

There are many forms of intermittent fasting with no concrete ways defined for you to do it. You just have to play around a little with your 'eating windows' and land on the methods that work the best for you. Below are some tips that you can work on practicing intermittent fasting:

The 12:12 Method

The 12:12 method allows you to eat a calory-controlled diet for 12 hours and fast for the next 12-hour window. One of the easiest ways to integrate it with your daily routine is to consume your dinner early and eat nothing after it. For the next meal (breakfast), make sure you give your stomach a 12-hour break!

The 16:8 Method

The 16:8 ratio of dieting allows the faster an 8-hour eating window with a buildup of 16 hours of fasting a day. For instance, if you are consuming your last meal of the day by 8 pm, you will eat nothing the next day until 2 in the noon.

The 5:2 Method

This diet is like a 24-hour fast and the alternate day fast in which we abstain from eating for 24 hours. But this one is quite convenient because we only need to fast twice a week for the whole day and eat normally for the rest of the five days.

24 Hour Method

This method requires you to restrict all food intake for an

entire day. You can practice this through either fasting once a week or going on fast on alternate days.

Is Fasting For Everyone? Who Should Avoid It?

While fasting is healthy and very fruitful for everyone, there are some uncertainties for people under certain conditions. For people who may suffer from medical issues should not fast for prolonged periods. No matter how beneficial autophagy is, it is not for everyone, and not everyone should jump on its bandwagon without prior consultation. The following are some scenarios where one should be cautious and preferably avoid partaking any fasting practices:

- Pregnant women
- Women planning to get pregnant
- Women who are breastfeeding
- People suffering from chronic diseases such as diabetes or cardiovascular diseases
- Diabetic patients with critical conditions

Pregnant women or women who are breastfeeding require a continuous intake of nutrients for which they should consume highly nutritious diets without strict restrictions on fats/calories or carbs.

Besides that, people who are suffering from diabetes may also avoid engaging in intermittent fasting for prolonged time durations. If you are someone who frequently feels dizzy and experiences the risk of falling, you should avoid fasting as well.

Consulting your doctor before adopting any diet plan will be a wiser option. Intermittent fasting or fasting for prolonged periods might not be a good idea for you to switch to instantly if you have a history of eating disorders.

"Restricting calorie intake can disrupt hormonal balance, leading to lower levels of estrogen and progesterone. And this can affect menstrual periods, fertility and mood," cautions Megan Wong, a registered dietitian.

What to Expect?

As per the research conducted by Whittel's with Jacksonville University, the results from autophagy should be prominent within two weeks. As per the eight weeks lasting lifestyle research, conducted by the team, the results proved to be the biomarkers (including body aft and skin complexion) as women ate certain foods and exercised.

The simplest way you can tell autophagy is working for you is by paying attention to how your body feels. "If you're starving during your fasting time, eat earlier than you planned and re-evaluate how much you're eating throughout the day. You may need more protein and fat in the meals you are eating," health and diet expert Presicci says.

And if you are feeling better, sleeping well, performing well at exercise and daily tasks with a sense of satisfaction, chances are, it is working for you!

Another way to know that it is working for you or what to expect of it is to find if you are aging well. If your progression is not in the reverse direction, i.e., from obesity to diabetes, then consider yourself on the right track and continue following the plan.

One of the great indicators of autophagy is your muscle building and stamina, which increases through autophagy. If you are not even building but just maintain your muscles, then you are probably dipping in the autophagy pathway. Other than some laboratory tests, it is difficult to know what's happening inside and how our body is performing in response to what mode we are setting it on. But if everything on the outside seems normal, then there is nothing to worry about. You are on the right track – the track to be healthy and fit. All you need to have is a motive to be better than you were yesterday and the determination to keep moving!

Chapter 16
The Conclusion

You do the hard work, stress out the same, and risk as much or more than other people when it comes to your fitness and health. Yet you notice a very slight change in your health progress and not the impact that should be created. Why does that happen?

Well, to give it to you straight, you may be missing out on the crucial details that can make or break your dietary patterns. We often sweep those minute details under the carpet or overlook them, not understanding how they might serve us. Here's what you need to do to generate the overall result for not just your physical but mental health: channel your efforts in the direction where they make an impact. And how are you going to do that? This is where my book will help you.

This book will be your guide and help you navigate the loopholes and mazes of the fitness processes. If we talk about prehistoric times, humans used to live in a very different food environment. Traditionally, humans in previous times were fasters and feasters. Although there was not a continuous flow of food supply, whenever they could arrange food, they would feast on it. Then there would be days that they would starve until they could feast on the other meal.

Fossil fuels are almost an ode to this eating pattern. They show the health and strength of prehistoric humans as their remains were found to be robust, with healthy teeth and bones, and very little to no signs of nutritional deficiency. This is understandable since they couldn't stroll through supermarket buying whole foods with all the specified dietary content. A fundamental aspect of early human life was to go without food from time to time.

Comparing this to the modern society, and the evolved surroundings that we live in, there's rarely a person today eating a modern industrial diet who goes long enough without food before consuming the next meal. Adding more to the problem is the ubiquity of processed foods and a sedentary lifestyle. With the advent of technology, humans have become so accustomed to digital facilities that we have restricted ourselves within a specific range. We indulge in fewer physical activities and stick to our digital devices for even our daily physical tasks. This book contains information about dietary patterns that you can adopt to sustain better health in modern society. Autophagy is one such process, as proved by Dr. Yoshinori Ohsumi. His research on the subject bagged him a Nobel award for this groundbreaking contribution to the health industry. Although autophagy has made its name with its many benefits outnumbering most of the previous health research and practices, there still a lot more to be studied. Autophagy will experience gain in attention as researchers conduct more studies on its impact on our health.

This book contains information stretched out on multiple disciplines and several associated pillars of autophagy. It discusses the methods to induce autophagy and how to incorporate it by taking baby steps in your current lifestyle. It also details its physical, mental, physiological, and psychological impact on the human body.

Autophagy is a long game and something that may require time. But it has a long-lasting impact. In the modern health paradigm, people are so misguided by the number of options available in the market that lead to deteriorating health in the name of body positivity. This book will help clear out the thick mist of confusion and will provide readers with guidelines on what autophagy is and how it can be used to detoxify and rebuild health.

I have kept the flow of the book easy to follow. I want everyone to understand the subject. One of the many reasons behind writing this book was the misguidance preached by the so-called big names. Because of my extensive research on the subject, I have designed this content precisely in chronological order, taking into account all the details and covering any loopholes.

The content in this book is the reflection of my lifestyle and encompasses an array of tips and techniques for you to adapt and avoid. With each chapter, as the book progresses, readers will get to know about health from a new perspective. The book preaches a lifestyle rather than a temporary diet pattern, which makes it different from other health books available in the market. This is because you need a permanent fix for your health, and I don't believe in just trimming the branches. Stay determined and stay healthy!

Happy autophagy!